REPRESENTATIVE NEBRASKANS

REPRESENTATIVE NEBRASKANS

By

J. R. JOHNSON, Ph.D.

Professor of History
State Teachers College, Wayne, Nebraska

Illustrated by

CLARENCE E. STRUBLE

JOHNSEN PUBLISHING COMPANY
LINCOLN, NEBRASKA

PRINTED IN THE UNITED STATES OF AMERICA
AMERICAN BOOK—STRATFORD PRESS, INC., NEW YORK

To My Wife
Frances Elizabeth
A Native Nebraskan

PREFACE

ONE HUNDRED YEARS AGO Nebraska became an organized territory. It stretched from the Missouri River on the east to the Rockies on the west; from Canada on the north to the Kansas border on the south. Within this vast area lived less than 3,000 white people. Today, with greatly reduced boundaries, Nebraska boasts a population of one and a third million inhabitants. A land once scorned as fit only for Indians and labeled the "Great American Desert" is now a thriving commonwealth with a proud history. Its residents take pride in calling themselves "Corn-huskers."

Prior to 1854 Nebraska's sparse population was made up largely of traders, trappers, soldiers, missionaries and Indians. The region was primarily a thoroughfare to the Far West. "Oh! California, that's the land for me, I'm going to Sacramento with a washbowl on my knee" was a hit tune. The trails to Oregon and Utah were heavy with travelers seeking the "Promised Land." But the hopes for sudden wealth faded. The dreams of weary migrants were shattered. Gradually the prairies and river valleys of Nebraska took on new meaning. The tune changed. "Let's stick to our farming and suffer no loss, for the stone that goes rolling doth gather no moss." Removal of the Indians, more liberal land policies and the coming of the railroad opened the door to new opportunities. "Gold is where you find it" and the plains of Nebraska proved to be a valuable source.

This little volume is intended as a means of revealing, through the lives of a number of representative Nebraskans, some of the history of the past one hundred years. This history makes a dramatic story. It is a story filled with joys and sorrows, of successes and failures. It is a story filled with exciting episodes. Many actors appear on the stage, some "big," some "little," but all necessary for unfolding the plot. It takes all kinds of people to build a state. Nebraska has been built by farmers, ranchers, business and professional men, and a host of others—as well as politicians. These sketches represent only a sampling from the great storehouse awaiting those who wish to delve into Nebraska biography.

Edgar Howard, long-haired editor of the *Columbus Telegram* and affectionately called the "Old Roman," once wrote: "How many colors does God hang in the sky when He paints a Nebraska sunset more beautiful than any other clime has known? I could not count the colors. . . . Last evening I witnessed a Nebraska sunset beyond compare. It was more beautiful than an artist's dream. Peering through the haze-clouds of uncertain hue the great orb of day flooded the landscape with a radiance of unspeakable beauty." Like Howard's sunset, it is impossible to "count the colors" that are painted on the historical canvas of Nebraska's past century—but they are legion. The panorama sometimes has been blurred by the "haze-clouds of uncertain hue," but the over-all picture is pleasing to most Cornhuskers.

This year, 1954, as Nebraskans celebrate their Territorial Centennial, I hope they will take the time to read more about the people who, each in his own way, have had a hand in the building of this great commonwealth. I shall feel greatly rewarded for my efforts if these thumbnail portraits help bring out some of the colors in the saga of Nebraska. I trust, too, that these sketches will stimulate the study of biography as a pleasant approach to history, especially among the young people of the state.

CONTENTS

CONTENTS

REPRESENTATIVE NEBRASKANS

CHRISTOPHER JOSEPH ABBOTT

Sandhills Rancher

OCTOBER 11, 1889 · JANUARY 10, 1954

GRANT COUNTY, located in the western part of Nebraska, boasts a population of 1,300 including at least six millionaires. At least ten others are worth a half-million each in terms of land and cattle. And these are the measuring sticks for wealth in the Sandhills. Hyannis, the county seat, population less than 500, was born in 1888 when the Burlington Railroad cut through the hills on its way into the Northwest. Here the early settlers soon discovered that the land was too rough and dry for farming but ideal for cattle raising with the grass growing as high as a horse and water holes abundant. Gold has been found in "them thar cattle" and since World War I the ranchers have enjoyed marked prosperity except during the Great Depression. Even then they fared better than most people. Almost all the ranchers are "comfortably fixed," a fact shown by the more than four million dollars in assets of the Bank of Hyannis.

[3]

Small ranches have been consolidated long since and large ranches, efficiently managed, are now in vogue. Many of these are comparable to the baronies of old, only modern conveniences make them the ultimate in up-to-date living. The main ranch house is usually a beautiful, white-painted mansion set in the middle of a landscaped garden. Spacious barns and machine sheds, all freshly painted, are found nearby. Roads are tortuous but the flivver plane gives the rancher quick transportation.

Top rancher and banker in Grant county until recently was colorful and "leathery" C. J. (Chris) Abbott whose land stretched over four counties. He was born near Bird City, Kansas, October 11, 1889, and came with his parents to a ranch near Hyannis the following year. He lived in the area his entire life and personified the character of that section of Nebraska. His grandfather homesteaded, his father increased the holdings and Chris added to them. Cattle ranching was his life. He described it as a "fascinating, wholesome and lucrative business." "There is," he wrote, "a variety in the work during the year and different from farming, as there are more activities scattered through the year. We have the haying or the harvesting of the wild hay in the summer, the shipping of the cattle in late summer and fall and the feeding of the cattle during the winter. We do no finish feeding here, but just the wild hay and cotton seed cake but no grain." Ranching is hard work but he liked it. For many years he was in the saddle every day galloping around his Sandhills domain taking a personal interest in the preparation of cattle for market.

Abbott attended the local schools and went through the tenth grade at Hyannis after which he enrolled at Nebraska Wesleyan Academy in University Place, Nebraska. He continued his studies at the University of Michigan and the University of Nebraska. He took courses in economics, law and engineering, all of which proved extremely useful to him. He earned athletic numerals in football at Michigan but did not engage in sports at Nebraska, probably figuring that he got plenty of exercise in the great outdoors. His comments on the need of an education for a ranching career are to the point.

"Often I am asked what amount of education a rancher should have for it is well known that many of our older and wealthy pioneers had little formal schooling. I feel that the amount of education that a person should have in order to be a successful ranch-

[4]

man would be hard to determine. There is never a time in a successful person's lifetime in which he is not being educated. The formal education that a boy might have upon leaving grammar school would be sufficient for a ranchman if he would educate himself as well as work. Self-education comes from reading books, by attending conventions, college programs, short courses in agriculture in the various universities, etc. My own experience is that I feel I have learned a great deal more since leaving college than I learned during the time I was in college. However, a minimum of education is necessary in order to create enough understanding so that you can progress in self-education."

He further stressed the need for agricultural training for ranch business. A knowledge of animal breeding and selection, according to Abbott, is indispensable in building up a herd, to know what one wants and how to get it. A business education is most helpful, for ranching is big business and involves much bookkeeping.

Abbott, as a young man, saw the need for good local banks as an aid to ranchers and for years was an organizer, director and office-holder in several of these throughout western Nebraska. He also had a financial interest in a variety of businesses and helped determine their policies. Lumber yards, livestock associations, banks, insurance companies, airways, railways and radio stations were only some of his varied interests in the business world. His travels were frequent and carried him to many meetings at scattered points. He flew his own plane on both business and pleasure trips to all parts of the country and he had his own landing strip.

Abbott was, indeed, a man of varied social and economic interests. He was active in Republican politics though he had no personal political ambitions. He just loved the "game." He listed his hobby as "Civic Work" and there is no doubt that he worked hard at his avocation. His business activities naturally brought him into close contact with innumerable social and civic affairs. Few developments in the Sandhills have been carried through without the Abbott touch. His influence reached far beyond state and regional limits. He has been a vice-president and director of the United States Chamber of Commerce, president of the Capitol Broadcasting Company, owner of Radio Station KFNF of Shenandoah, Iowa, vice president of the American National Livestock Association, chairman of the Board of Transportation of New York and, of course, president of the Abbott Company of Hyannis. The Abbotts owned as many as a dozen banks in western Nebraska and Chris served as president of most of them. He was a director of the Mutual Benefit, Health and Accident Association of Omaha; Northwestern Bell Telephone Company, Omaha; Omaha National Bank and the Union Stockyards Company in the same city.

But Chris Abbott's interests were not confined to the business field. He held memberships in the Masonic Lodge, Elks, Ak-Sar-Ben, Omaha Athletic Club and many other organizations of a civic nature. He was a delegate to the 1948 and 1952 Republican National Conventions and favored Thomas E. Dewey and Douglas MacArthur for the Presidency. Abbott married Helen Sears of Denver, Colorado, in 1914 and they had a son and two daughters. Following her death he married Ethel Schmitz Page in 1933. The Abbott home stands at the outskirts of Hyannis, a large two-story red brick structure and furnished as luxuriously as any residence in a large city. This was headquarters for Christopher Abbott and here he led a busy life until his recent tragic death. His directorships and other affairs took him away from the active work on the ranch but, in his own words: "I do not think that I will ever completely give up seeing to the shipping and building up of the herd." He spoke of the future of ranching as a "sure thing." His predictions should mean something for he talked out of long experience. He had followed ranching first-hand through periods of boom and depression. "As long as people eat," he commented, "they will want beef and they will select beef perhaps in preference to any other food." No doubt about it—beef will ever be the All-American favorite whether in the form of a T-bone steak or ground into hamburger.

Nebraskans were shocked recently when a news flash announced the death of Chris Abbott in a plane crash near Shreveport, Louisiana. He and eleven other prominent men were returning from a duck-hunting trip on the Louisiana marshlands near the Gulf Coast when their private seaplane crashed and burned. Chris had once jokingly explained his technique for flying an airplane. "To land," he said, "you just fly close to the spot you want, pull back on the stick, close your eyes and pray. It's always worked for me." This time, however, he was not handling the stick. The career of the man reputed to be Nebraska's wealthiest citizen was ended abruptly. Sixty business associates and friends including the mayor of Omaha, went by special train to Hyannis to attend his funeral at the Congregational Church. One of these, Albert A. Held of Lincoln, described Mr. Abbott as "an aggressive, honest-to-God citizen." But one of the ranchers summed up the general feeling of his neighbors when he said: "People didn't realize how big a man he was until after he was gone."

Christopher Abbott was no genius but he was a good solid citizen who did much to advance the interests of his beloved Sandhills as well as the state as a whole. He did not squander his inheritance as many have done but took his "starts" and developed these to new and higher levels. He kept pace with changing conditions and utilized new techniques as they appeared. In advancing his own interests he aided others. In conjunction with his neighbors he proved that the Sandhills country is a good place to build homes and find prosperity. Grinnell College of Grinnell, Iowa, at its commencement exercises June 7, 1953, conferred upon him an honorary degree of Doctor of Laws for his outstanding contributions in pasture and dryland farming and beef cattle breeding. Abbott's career may not be set down as a spectacular one but it is worthy of study. This leading rancher and banker of the Sandhills has shown by example what can be accomplished by a steady purpose, hard work and just plain, everyday, good common sense.

GRACE ABBOTT

Social Worker

NOVEMBER 17, 1878 · JUNE 19, 1939

GRACE ABBOTT once remarked: "The only way to elevate the condition of the child is to elevate the family. Whatever the parents have is passed on to their children. If we want the children to have more we must see that the parents have more. We can depend on the parents to care for their own." And again she declared: "You can't feed children skim milk this year and make up to them by feeding them cream next year. Neither can you make up to them tomorrow for the neglect, the suffering, the abuse heaped upon them today." Herein lies much of the philosophy of one of Nebraska's most outstanding women who preferred to be known as "social worker and educator of social workers."

The first conference of all the states for child welfare was called by President Hoover in 1930 to meet at the White

[8]

House. Miss Abbott, then Chief of the Children's Bureau, not only presided over the meeting but was very active in its work. She learned that a congressional committee was planning to recommend that the Children's·Bureau be blanketed into the United States Public Health Service. Should this happen she feared that the economic, legal and health program for children which had been developed would be lost. The report was to be considered in a room that would hold only fifty people. When the time came two hundred angry delegates were on hand and the meeting was shifted to Constitution Hall. It was an excited gathering. Miss Abbott sat quietly through the rumpus. Though she never admitted it, the rumors were that she had been on the telephone all night making long-distance calls. Telegrams streamed in from all over the nation. Needless to say, the report was defeated.

Miss Abbott came from sturdy stock, one of Nebraska's eminent families. She was born in Grand Island, Nebraska, November 17, 1878. Her father, O. A. Abbott, was a pioneer lawyer, state senator, first lieutenant governor of the state, a member of Nebraska's first and second constitutional conventions and a veteran of the Civil War. Her mother, Elizabeth Griffin Abbott, was a noted pioneer in the educational field. Young Grace had the advantages of a good home environment and at the same time witnessed the hardships of pioneer life such as droughts, crop failures, blizzards and grasshoppers. After attending the Grand Island public schools she enrolled in Grand Island College, a Baptist school, graduating with a Bachelor of Philosophy degree in 1898. After a year of study at the University of Nebraska she taught in the Grand Island High School for several years, 1899 to 1902, 1903 to 1907. She instructed at Mt. Holyoke College the school year 1902 to 1903.

She now joined her sister Edith, who was a resident of Hull House in Chicago and doing social service work. Henceforth Grace's life was thoroughly dedicated to social work, especially as it affected women and children. Nine years were spent as a director of the Immigrants Protective League, an organization to protect newly arrived immigrants from exploitation and aid them in becoming adjusted to life in America. During this time she studied at the University of Chicago, receiving the Master of Philosophy degree in political science in 1909. In addition she taught a course in immigration and lectured to various groups. Her services continued to be much in demand. She held offices as secretary, director and consultant in various welfare organizations inside and outside of the government. Under her direction many investigations and studies were made, both on the state and national levels which served as a basis for welfare legislation. She was a consultant to the War Policies Board. Presidents and governors sought her counsel.

In 1921 Miss Abbott was selected by President Harding to succeed Julia C. Lathrop as Chief of the United States Children's Bureau, an agency with which she was already associated and had done much to develop. She held this post until 1934, during which time much progress was made "in assembling uniform child welfare statistics, particularly of juvenile delinquency and child labor." Under her direction more funds were appropriated for this work and during the period, 1921 to 1930, more than 75 investigations were made in 35 states, the District of Columbia and Puerto Rico. Intensive research in laws affecting children in various states and foreign countries furnished valuable information on which to build a program of action. Miss Abbott met with constant opposition from industries employing child labor and saw her work slowed down by adverse constitutional decisions.

Hardly had she taken over the post when she began to urge the passage of a bill that would coordinate federal and state aid for mothers and children. The result was the Sheppard-Towner Act, the enforcement of which was under the direction of her bureau. She kept an all-out publicity campaign going during her administration, using every means available: exhibits, motion pictures, radio talks and bulletins. Four million copies of the pamphlets "Prenatal Care," "Infant Care," "Child Care," and "Child Management" were distributed. Two bulletins, "Standards for Physicians Conducting Conferences in Child Health Centers" and "Standards of Prenatal Care—An Outline for the Use of Physicians" were issued in 1928. Miss Abbott pulled no punches. Saving mothers and babies was more important, she contended, than raising better crops and livestock.

Shortly after becoming Chief she was selected by the Department of State, on invitation of the League of Nations, to serve in an advisory and consultative capacity as our member of the League's advisory committee on traffic in women and children. Miss Abbott attended the meetings in Geneva in 1923 and 1925 where her suggestions were well received. One marvels at the energy of this woman. While heading the Bureau she managed to find the time to serve as Professor of Public Welfare and edit *Social Service* at the University of Chicago. Her untiring efforts focused the attention of the public on problems that too many ignored in an era when everyone 'seemed to want to live "high, wide and handsome."

Miss Abbott wrote several books and contributed to many magazines. Among her books are: *The Immigrant and his Community, The Immigrant in Mass, The Immigrant and the Mines, The Girl and Society,* and *Public Assistance.* She wrote for a definite purpose, to present the facts and stimulate governmental action. Though labeled a pacifist she supported Franklin D. Roosevelt because she believed in his social welfare program. By 1930 her name was familiar to every club, college and civic organization throughout the country because of her welfare work. She was credited with knowing and caring more about the fifty-three million children than anyone else in the United States. That same year the *Good Housekeeping Magazine* conducted a National Poll to select the Nation's twelve most distinguished women. Miss Abbott was ranked only second to Jane Addams, the woman whose inspiration had started her on a career of social welfare. The University of New Hampshire conferred the honorary degree of Doctor of Laws on her in 1931 and Wisconsin in 1932.

Miss Abbott saw the fruits of her pioneering in human welfare in the social legislation of the Thirties. In a period that witnessed a new emphasis on conservation of our natural resources a new bill of rights was, likewise, written for the "forgotten man." Raising the standard of living for the workers elevated the family and brought to underprivileged children the advantages which Grace Abbott had fought for during her entire, unselfish lifetime. Child labor laws, which in an earlier period were set aside as unconstitutional by the Supreme Court, now were upheld by a more liberal group of jurists. Nebraska should be proud of this woman who contributed so much to the advancement of human welfare.

GROVER CLEVELAND ALEXANDER

Baseball Immortal

FEBRUARY 26, 1887 · NOVEMBER 4, 1950

THIRTY-NINE is considered old in the baseball world, but Grover Cleveland Alexander, Old Pete, as he was affectionately called by his fans, won his greatest triumph at that "ripe" old age. He did it in Yankee Stadium, the "House that Babe Ruth built." It was the crucial seventh game of the 1926 World Series when the mighty Yanks and the St. Louis Cards were slugging it out right down to the end of the string.

Alex had been released by the Chicago Cubs because he mixed too much whiskey with his baseball and apparently showed no indication of changing his habits. Roger Hornsby, manager of the Cards, exacted no pledges from Old Pete except that he be able to "deliver the goods" when he took his turn on the mound. This he did in an exemplary fashion.

Alex had already won two games in this Series, including the sixth, leaving the standing at three apiece. Surely he had done his part and was entitled to do a bit of celebrating. This was the prohibition era but it was not difficult to find the "right" places. Accounts vary on Old Pete's nocturnal adventure. Some contend he got gloriously drunk and, therefore, was unfit for further pitching duties. He denies this and one is inclined to believe his story. Whatever the truth, his past escapades rose up to plague him.

The seventh game was on Sunday and a pitching duel was in progress between Waite Hoyt of the Yanks and Jess Haines of the Cards. A run in the sixth inning brought the score to three to two in favor of St. Louis. As the seventh inning came up, the New York "Murderers' Row" faced the pitcher and soon loaded the bases—with two out. "Poosh-'em-up" Tony Lazzeri stepped to the plate. The situation was tense. Hornsby had to make a quick decision. Haines was handicapped with a bleeding finger tip and it seemed advisable to take him out. Two relief pitchers were warming up in the "bull pen." There had been a drizzle all morning and there was a chill in the air. Alexander felt that chill while sitting on the bench so went out and joined them to get warmed up. To the surprise of the crowd (and perhaps Old Pete), Hornsby, playing at second base, gave Alexander the sign to take over. He ambled in slowly as he afterwards related, to keep young Lazzeri "pawing the earth awhile." Those who saw him thought he was in an alcoholic fog. Actually his head was clear as crystal. Hornsby met him and looking into his eyes spoke confidence. "You can do it, Pete."

The crowd, only half-size because of the weather, roared as Alexander threw a few warm-up pitches. All over the country radio fans listened intently. The first pitch was a ball, the second a strike, but on the third throw the clock stood still. Tony connected for what looked like a home run but it went foul. It was a dramatic moment that next pitch. Old Pete gave it all he had and Lazzeri, poised for the kill, swung mightily—and missed.

"So sudden and complete was the release of tension that fans to this day seem to remember that the game ended right there. Actually, there were two more innings, but the Yankees did not threaten again. The final out came when Babe Ruth, who had been purposely handed a base on balls, was caught trying to steal second."

Old Pete said he got three thrills that day; the first was fanning Lazzeri, the second when Hornsby tagged Ruth trying to steal second and the third when Commissioner Landis handed him a check for $5,584.51, winner's share. But, his dramatic appearance and performance in that crucial game will thrill baseball fans as long as the game is played. Thousands of writers have immortalized it "and it will continue to be reconstructed and retold again and again down the ages in the spirit of the ancient Roman epic of 'Horatius at the Bridge.' " After this feat there seemed to be "no more worlds for him to conquer."

Grover Cleveland Alexander, the modern "Alexander the Great," is Nebraska's greatest contribution to baseball. He played with the Phillies from 1911 to 1917, with the Cubs 1918 to 1926, the Cards 1926 to 1929 and finished out with the Phillies in 1930. He got his last big tribute in 1938 when voted into baseball's Hall of Fame at Cooperstown, New York.

He was born in St. Paul, Nebraska, February 26, 1887. As a small boy his thoughts turned to baseball and he never turned down an opportunity to play the game. He had little interest in farming or for that matter in any settled occupation. The local denizens undoubtedly thought him to be a worthless and shiftless young man. But he knew what he wanted to do—play baseball. While displaying his pitching wares on a local club against a traveling team he was spotted by a scout and his chance had come. His first appearance in organized baseball was as a pitcher for Galesburg, Illinois, in the Illinois-Missouri League in 1909. Next season he worked for Syracuse in the New York State League and then was acquired by the Phillies. Alexander had started his conquests. At Philadelphia he came under the coaching tutelage of Pat Moran who taught him many fine points of the game. In three years, 1915–1917, he won 95 games. Four of his wins in 1915 were one-hit games, an all-time record. He never had a no-hitter. A summary of his remarkable feats may seem prosaic but it is certainly revealing.

1. Pitched more National League games (696) and won more National League games (373) than any other pitcher in history.
2. Led his League in number of complete games pitched, a major league record shared only by Walter Johnson.
3. Earned run average of 1.22 is the National League record for pitchers working in 250 innings or more.
4. National League record for number of years leading the League

by earned run average and also games won . . . 5 times he led by the ERA and 6 times in the won and lost column.

5. Only National League pitcher that ever led the League in both won and lost percentage and ERA in 2 different games.
6. Pitched 90 shutouts, the lifetime National League record.
7. Sixteen shutouts in 1916 set the present major league record for one year.
8. Pitched 4 successive shutouts his first year, 1911. Shares the record with Ed Reulbach.

Alexander was called in the draft in April, 1918, after pitching the opening game for the Cubs. He reported to Camp Funston and was attached to the 89th Division, 342nd Field Artillery. He was made a sergeant and transferred to Camp Mills. In early July he went overseas and was in action in the Met Sector until September. Following the Armistice he served with the Army of Occupation in Germany until the following March and was honorably discharged upon his arrival in New York.

There is little point in following the mistakes of Old Pete after he left the major league. His principal enemy, John Barleycorn, continued to dog his footsteps. He and his wife, Aimee, were divorced. Like many others who have reached the heights of fame and fortune he did not save for a rainy day. But he was not and will not be forgotten. His last appearance in a major league uniform on a major league field was September 1, 1936, on the occasion of the St. Louis celebration of the 60th anniversary of the National League. Sam Breadon re-assembled his 1926 Cardinals and with Old Pete in the pitcher's box played an exhibition game with the 1936 Cardinals. It was an impressive scene and the spotlight centered on the man with the unmatched 19-year pitching career.

This one-time stormy figure of big-league baseball died in virtual obscurity in a rented room in St. Paul, Nebraska, November 4, 1950.

> "But fame is fleeting as the wind,
> And glory fades away."

Only about 150 people were on hand to see him off to join the Valhalla ball club, including his divorced wife and his three brothers. Just a few weeks before, through the efforts of a hometown friend, Old Pete was given a last wish—to go to New York and see part of the World Series between the Yanks and the

Phillies. He had been living on a $100 monthly pension supplemented by a government disability check. The baseball allotment was provided by a fund set up by the late Sam Breadon, owner of the St. Louis Cards. This organization also paid all funeral expenses. Alex thought all along that his pension check came from National League funds.

Bill Corum paid high tribute to the great baseball player in his column:

"I watched and wrote about Johnson, Shocker, Faber, Quinn, the subtle Pennock, the smooth Art Nehf, mighty Vance, the stubble-chinned Grimes, Hoyt and Ruffing, the remarkable Gomez, Grove, Luque, Rowe, Lyons, Wyatt, Fitzsimmons, Rommell, Earnshaw, Derringer, Carlson, Hallihan, Chandler, Dean, Newsom, Hughson, Feller, and Grover Cleveland Alexander. And of all of these, if anybody had told me to take one pitcher for one game that you must win, I would have put the finger on Alexander—To me he had it all. Everything a great pitcher could have, including most of all, that priceless asset of the real pitcher—pin point control."

Old Pete may not have controlled his private life too well but he certainly knew how to control a baseball. To quote Bill Corum again, Grover Cleveland Alexander was the "greatest pitcher to wrap his fingers around a new white ball." In the years to come when baseball pitchers are praised, the old timers will say: "Yeah, but you should have seen Ol' Pete."

JONAS L. BRANDEIS

Merchant Deluxe

NOVEMBER 14, 1836 · JANUARY 23, 1903

BRANDEIS STORE is more than display counters, show cases, piles of merchandise and escalators. It is more than steel and stone. It is a city within a city. It is an institution built on integrity and years of service. "Get it at Brandeis" is a common expression and many a shopper has done all his buying there without setting foot in another store. "Just as the ancients with their beasts of burden trudged to the market places at Rome and Athens, thousands of persons now gather at the market place of the great Middlewest—Brandeis." It is the Marshall Field of Omaha where people meet, greet, eat and buy their needs—and luxuries. If it isn't satisfactory, return it. The customer is always right.

Brandeis employs over 1,200 people and another 500 to meet the Christmas rush. Its 104 selling departments and 34 nonselling departments are spread over ten floors and 408,692 square feet of floor space. More than 10 million people pass through its doors annually. The entire population of Omaha could be carried on its escalators one story in four hours. Over 250 miles of yard goods are sold in one year. Four million, one-hundred eighty three thousand paper bags, 650,000 boxes and 18,000 reams of gift tissue are one year's supply in serving its customers. The Brandeis Cafeteria and Pompeian Room serve some two million people annually. More than 40,000 customers have charge accounts at Brandeis. Fifty-six buyers comb the world for new merchandise and buy from more than half the 48 states in the Union. Its power plant furnishes heat for 22 downtown buildings. Within the building is a laundry, print shop, postoffice, bank, two restaurants and innumerable shops. One thousand telephones are in use. Air-conditioning makes shopping a pleasant pastime in the hot summer months. A 534-car parking garage is conveniently located for its customers' use.

These statistics tell a story of modern efficiency, of stream-lined service that meet the demands of the busy shopper of today. One may wonder what makes Brandeis the great merchandising mecca of the Midwest. It did not just happen. It is the result of the inspiration of its founder, Jonas L. Brandeis, who opened a one-room store in Omaha in 1881, and to the policies of his successors. Keeping pace in an ever-changing business world when thousands of early day stores dropped by the wayside has paid dividends. The motto of Jonas L. Brandeis, "Give the same goods for less money—or better goods for the same money," continues to be the boast of the Store.

The founder of the House of Brandeis was born in 1836 in Prague, Bohemia, then a part of the Hapsburg empire of Austria. At the age of 17 he came to Milwaukee, Wisconsin. His career reads like a Horatio Alger story. After taking a bride he moved to Manitowac where he started a small business and sold goods to the settlers in this frontier village. Here his four children, a daughter and three sons, were born. His sons were initiated into the art of merchandising. Sensing the significance of Omaha, Nebraska, as the Gateway to the West, Brandeis decided to locate there. In the fall of 1881 he unloaded his family, and such possessions as could be transported, from the Missouri River ferry at Omaha. Frontier conditions still prevailed here. Though the railroad had wrought many changes it was still an outfitting place for those making the long haul across the plains with wagons. Omaha was without paved streets or electric lights and had had a telephone exchange only two years.

Brandeis was eager to get into harness. He opened the Fair Store at 506 South Thirteenth Street in December. His displays of merchandise in the windows and on the sidewalk attracted attention and he soon had a thriving business. He sold quality goods at reasonable prices and the service left nothing to be desired. Volume business brought him fair profits at reduced prices. It has been said that Brandeis Store managers "have invariably believed that the first, second, and third parts of successful merchandising is Action, and they have never failed to act in accordance with their belief." Jonas Brandeis set that pattern. Competition spurred him on. His methods were something of a jolt to his competitors. "He kept his windows lighted at nights. He studded his newspaper ads with pictures. On Saturday nights he released a dozen balloons, each carrying a coupon good for a free suit of clothes." He was constantly seeking out novel ways of attracting customers. When holding a big sale he would send his young sons out driving a sale wagon loaded with bargains, bearing plainly marked price tags. The Fair, in these ways, was made known to every part of the city as a bargain center.

The record from here on is one of expansion, expansion and more expansion. First it was renting an adjoining store room followed shortly with leasing the whole building, a three-story structure at the southwest corner of Thirteenth and Howard streets. The three sons, Arthur, Emil and Hugo, learned merchandising from top to bottom and were not only of great assistance to their enterprising father but, in later years, were able to step in and promote the House of Brandeis to metropolitan dimensions.

Jonas Brandeis planned carefully before making the next step. After seven years it was decided to move the store to a central, uptown location, so in 1888 the Fair became the Boston Store at 114 South Sixteenth street. Business continued to increase and Mr. Brandeis, with an eye on the future, proceeded to purchase ground at the northwest corner of Sixteenth and Douglas, where a four-story structure soon made its appearance. A partnership was formed under the name of J. L. Brandeis & Sons and the Boston Store now became the busiest spot in Omaha. This was 1891 and in spite of a nation-wide depression in 1893, the store did a big business.

Early in 1894 the Boston Store was destroyed by fire. Losses, store 50 thousand dollars, stock 150 thousand dollars, were covered by only 160 thousand dollars insurance. In addition much of the family silver and jewelry was lost in the flames. Undaunted, the Brandeis clan got busy, leased the Bell Department Store at Fifteenth and Dodge and proceeded to carry on business "as usual." An announcement was made that a new structure would be built on the old site. Extra ground was purchased adjoining the old corner and a building twice the size of the former store graced the landscape before the end of the year.

Jonas L. Brandeis died in 1903 but the institution he founded has continued to flourish and stands as a monument memorializing his business acumen and faith in the Midwest. Thousands of early-day stores fell by the wayside but the House that Jonas built, like Old Man River, just keeps rollin' along. His enterprising sons, schooled in the principles of the founder, kept pace with an accelerated age. In 1906 they erected an eight-story structure on the south side of Douglas street between Sixteenth and Seventeenth streets. The name was now changed to the Brandeis Store. In 1921 two additional stories were added. George Brandeis, a nephew of Jonas L., ultimately became chief of all the Brandeis interests following the death of Arthur, last surviving son.

George, like his illustrious uncle, was an immigrant. He spent two years in the Thirteenth street store and for many years was employed by the Boston Store in Chicago. Later he was made assistant manager in Omaha by Arthur Brandeis and advanced to general manager. In addition to his keen business acumen, he was active in all public affairs and helped promote such projects as the Fontenelle Hotel, Medical Arts Building, Omaha Athletic Club, and the Omaha Elks. It has been said that "no public enterprise, in any way worthy of support, has ever failed receiving from the Brandeis interests the aid that it deserved."

If Jonas L. Brandeis could return to Omaha and see the new Brandeis Store with its bubbling activity, he might be a bit surprised but probably not shocked. He would, undoubtedly, approve all the changes made to serve the ever-increasing demands of the buying public. He would, likewise, note with pride that his maxim is still being followed: "Give the same goods for less money—or better goods for the same money." A recent advertisement comments: "Yes, we've grown a lot since 1881. We've grown from a one-room retail store without electric lights, auto delivery cars, elevators, charga-plates, or even telephones," but "we are still young and are still growing. We don't want to rest on past achievements— In the future, as in the past, our constant endeavor will be to live up to our founder's original policy: To maintain a complete assortment of finest merchandise marked at moderate prices."

HERBERT BROWNELL, JR.

Political Strategist

FEBRUARY 20, 1904

———◆◉◆———

UNDOUBTEDLY MOST AMERICANS are aware that Herbert Brownell, Jr. is now Attorney General of the United States and hence a member of President Eisenhower's Cabinet. Students have learned this fact in their government classes. His name appears almost daily in the newspapers, magazines carry articles on him and news commentators frequently point up his vigorous actions on radio and TV. The recent revelations on the Harry Dexter White case prove that he is alert to the Communist menace and have brought him both praise and ridicule. His concrete proposals for new security measures to strengthen the investigative arm of the Department of Justice assure us that he is doing everything possible to maintain our national security. Brownell has been called the "second most powerful man in the United States."

When President-elect Eisenhower went to Korea, in fulfillment of a campaign pledge, he took along two of his future Cabinet members, Charles Wilson, Secretary of Defense designate and Herbert Brownell, Jr., his choice for Attorney General. It was understandable that Wilson should go but the latter seemed an illogical choice. He knew little of military or production problems nor was he too well informed on foreign policy. Why, then, did Ike take Brownell? This posed the "64-dollar" question. Robert Wallace, writing in *Life*, gave the answer.

"The answer lies in what Brownell carries around in his large and wispy-haired head. He is a highly intelligent man who is able to make rapid and very sound judgments even about things with which he may at the outset be unfamiliar. Brownell is a human thinking machine and can think not alone in terms of things as they appear but as they might be. One or two of the men around Eisenhower may be more intelligent than Brownell, several may be more sophisticated, some on occasion may make sounder judgments; but as an all-around man, as an intellectual political utility infielder, Brownell is without equal."

Herbert Brownell, Jr. first came into national prominence in 1944 when he managed the political campaign of Governor Thomas E. Dewey for the Presidency. But the name Brownell has long been a familiar one in Nebraska. Herbert Brownell, Sr. was for 17 years a professor of physical science at Peru (Nebraska) State Teachers College and for 26 years was associated with Teachers College at the University of Nebraska. Here he organized and headed the Department of Science and later was made Head of the Department of Secondary Education. His efforts were directed chiefly toward the training of teachers for secondary schools. He authored several science textbooks widely used in Nebraska and the Middlewest. It was in this academic atmosphere that Herbert Jr. and his four sisters and two brothers grew up.

The Brownell family was an institution on the University of Nebraska campus. In 1933 Professor and Mrs. Brownell were named "father and mother of the Nebraska Innocents and scholarship." The Innocents society is a senior honorary organization and forms the "hard core" of campus politics. All three of the Brownell boys were members. Several years later Mrs. Brownell was presented the Lincoln Kiwanis Club's gold medal for distinguished service to the state as a "mother, homemaker, citizen and gracious lady." Science Education scholarships were set up at the University in honor of Professor Brownell. One of the new Attorney General's brothers, Dr. Samuel Brownell, is now United States Commissioner of Education. Without a doubt the Brownell family has contributed much to the advancement of the state and the nation—and the influence continues.

Herbert, Jr. was born in the little town of Peru, Nebraska, on February 20, 1904. At the age of six he moved with the family to Lincoln where he grew to manhood. Frugality was a household trait and Herb worked at various jobs when not in school. At an early age he became intrigued with politics and acquainted himself with the offices, candidates and issues. Collecting campaign cards was a hobby. He was not the athletic type but was active in many other school activities. At Lincoln High School he managed the school paper, was president of the debating club and served as class president. At the University his interest in politics was stepped up but he chose to remain in the background and "cook up" schemes for the campus campaigns. As a manager this capable, soft-spoken, pleasant young man was superb. His abilities were quickly recognized and put to use. Herb edited the *Daily Nebraskan,* was chosen president of the journalism fraternity and was a member of Delta Upsilon social fraternity. He was selected by popular vote as one of "the 10 most representative Nebraska students" in the Class of 1924.

When Brownell graduated Phi Beta Kappa at the age of 20 he was torn between two desires, to study journalism or law. He applied for scholarships at the Columbia School of Journalism and the Yale Law School. The latter school made the better offer and there he enrolled. He made an enviable record and was editor of the *Law Review,* a post which traditionally went to the top man in the class. He roomed with brother Samuel who was taking postgraduate work at Yale. During vacation periods the two young men traveled around the country in an old Model-T Ford. This was the era when "See America First" was the slogan.

Brownell was graduated cum laude from the Yale Law School in 1927. He was about to return to Lincoln to practice when an offer came from the prominent Wall Street law firm of Root, Clark, Buckner, Howland and Ballantine to serve as a law clerk. Emory R. Buckner of the firm was a graduate of the University of Nebraska, Class of 1904, and extended the invitation. He made a wise decision in accepting, for it gave him his chance to crash "Big Time" and make full use of his legal powers. He spent two years with this office then transferred to Lord, Day and Lord, a long established conservative firm. He proved his worth and within three years was made a member of the organization. His association here lasted until he became Attorney General twenty years later.

Almost from the time he set foot in New York City Brownell was active in practical politics. He knew one must start at the bottom and "learn the ropes." He joined a Young Republican Club and was put to work "hewing wood and carrying water." His bailwick was the old gerrymandered Tenth Assembly District. No better political laboratory could have been found for a young man eager to grapple with an assortment of people and problems. This constituency included Greenwich Village, Gramercy Park and the garment and theater districts. Here, too, Brownell met a young man from Michigan, Tom Dewey, also trying his luck in the big city. The two became close friends and the association continues to this day.

New York City was hardly a political featherbed for aspiring young Republicans. These were depression years and Republicans were not held in high esteem generally. However, corruption ran rampant in the metropolis as the Seabury investigations disclosed. Brownell and Dewey teamed up, determined to whip the Tammany Hall crowd in the Tenth District. In 1931 the former ran for the State Assembly and the latter managed his campaign. Running for office was a new experience for Brownell and an enlightening one. Though defeated he kept plugging away and the following year was victorious despite the Roosevelt landslide. He continued to represent the Tenth District until 1937 when he withdrew voluntarily to devote more time to his neglected law practice and to his family. Brownell had married Doris McCarter of Dublin, Texas, a social service worker, in 1934. Today the Brownells have a family of two girls and two boys.

The young attorney made a commendable record in the Legislature. He sponsored a number of reform measures including a bill to provide New York City a new charter. This was a "must" for bringing about a reorganization of its government along business-like lines. The City's finances were in a mess and drastic action was imperative in face of a bankrupt situation. Tom Dewey as a special prosecutor was going "great guns" with his racket-busting activities. Brownell was his strong right arm in the Legislature pushing the legislation needed by the racket-buster. Other of his measures were a child-labor law and a bill setting up minimum wage standards.

Brownell's internship in politics taught him, more than ever, the value of effective organization and teamwork. He used intelligent members of the Young Republican Club as scouts to seek out other capable young men. A card file was kept on each voter and special efforts were made to "convert" the wavering ones in the middle. Ever the realist he recognized the importance of making personal contacts and giving responsibility to those with brains and character. When he left the Legislature Brownell did not forsake politics but his future role was to be that which he loved best—managing campaigns. In 1941 he managed, at Dewey's behest, the campaign of his friend Edgar J. Nathan, Jr., who ran successfully for President of New York City's Borough of Manhattan. This was only the beginning. He directed Dewey's gubernatorial race in 1942 and his candidate won by nearly 650,000 votes. Brownell became a key man at Albany. The following year he managed Joe R. Hanley's successful campaign for Lieutenant Governor but the "big deal" came when he was selected to manage Dewey's bid for the Presidency in 1944. He went into the campaign with characteristic vigor and applied all the organizational and promotional techniques at his command. It was a hard fight and a tough one to lose. They were up against the "Champ" and—"there was a war on."

Brownell remained Chairman of the Republican National Committee until March, 1946, picking up the "loose ends" and laying plans for the next election. He resigned to have more time for his legal practice. He was General Counsel for the American Hotel Association as well as the New York State and City Hotel Associations. A specialist in business law his services were in great demand. Brownell had helped plan the New York World's Fair and was Vice Chairman of the Commission. As chief counsel for the Fair he had a remarkable batting average losing only one case out of more than a thousand suits brought against the organization.

Always ready to back Tom Dewey, Brownell returned to manage his campaign for the Presidency in 1948. Many Republican leaders thought that Harry Truman would be a "push-over" but Dewey's manager did not share this optimism. He could see storm signals and warned them that it would be a close election but they assured him that it was "in the bag." He tape recorded some of their optimism and played it back to them later but they didn't relish his sense of humor. Some "passed the buck" and said he had botched up the campaign. Many individuals would have become discouraged to the point of withdrawing forever from politics but not Brownell. He was not ready to flee to the "tall timber." Instead he bounced back in 1952 to take a leading part in the Eisenhower play. Dewey had come out for Ike who was then Commander of SHAPE. Brownell flew to Paris and had some serious talks with the General. He came back satisfied that Ike would run and with a belief that his abilities reached far beyond the military field. Also, it appears that the General was greatly impressed with the worth of this fellow-midwesterner.

Since Brownell was indelibly stamped as a Dewey man it seemed best that he remain behind the scenes as much as possible. But he had a major part in "putting over" Ike's nomination. His strategy helped save the Texas vote in the Convention. He burned up the wires at Chicago making the right contacts. After the Convention he seemed to drop from sight but reappeared when a crucial decision had to be made. He was in on the parley in St. Louis that decided how the Nixon case should be handled. Shortly before election day he slipped into Ike's headquarters in Denver. Just what took place is none too clear but we do know that it was Brownell who advised giving the Korean issue greater emphasis in the campaign. During the home stretch he kept busy on the telephone "directing and counselling" in true Brownellian fashion.

Now Herbert Brownell, Jr., heads the "biggest law firm in the world," the Department of Justice. He is taking his job seriously and during his one year as Attorney General has wrought notable changes. *Nation's Business* makes this report:

"Attorney General Brownell took charge with a sure and firm hand. This was made plain when he named excellent lawyers as assistant attorneys general and as heads of the several divisions in the Department. These men quickly won each other's respect, and demonstrated capacity for teamwork. The atmosphere in the Department was cleared up within a few months. The restoration of morale was dramatic. The Department began functioning once again like a first-class law office. This was a great contribution to the administration of Government."

Brownell is probably the President's chief dispenser of patronage. But patronage, in the Attorney General's dictionary, is not a foul word. Party loyalty is a consideration but loyalty to the Government is more important. He believes in getting men with ability and whose integrity is unquestioned. At his suggestion the Republican party, even before election, engaged a management consultant firm to check the qualifications needed for filling a thousand offices. In a recent address to the law students at the University of Texas Brownell stressed the need for "top-flight lawyers" for the Department of Justice. "We will," he said, "make available each year 30 positions in the department to be filled by the best qualified law graduates who apply for jobs. Selections will be strictly on the basis of merit. We will seek to obtain law graduates from all areas, and not from one geographical segment of the nation. The starting salary will be competitive with that offered by the large law firms."

Herbert Brownell, Jr. is no "stuffed shirt." He is a good mixer. He likes parties and his favorite sport is baseball, especially when the Yanks are playing. The family often vacations at a ranch in Arizona and he is considered a fair horseman. He likes the great outdoors and hunting is one of his diversions. Brownell is still a youthful looking man, not particularly colorful, but he can flash a broad smile that is infectious. He is an excellent and convincing speaker and his quiet sense of humor stands him in well. He can laugh at his own mistakes. This Midwesterner has achieved much in his fifty years. He has added lustre to the Brownell name and to his native state.

WILLIAM JENNINGS BRYAN

Crusader

MARCH 19, 1860 · JULY 26, 1925

FOR MANY YEARS the name Bryan was almost synonomous with the name Nebraska. Few developments of importance took place in the Middlewest, or the Nation for that matter, without bringing comment from the Great Commoner. He had arrived in Lincoln in 1887 where he settled down to practice law. But the law office was too confining for William Jennings Bryan. Almost immediately he was caught up in the political whirl to which he offered little resistance. The very next year he was a delegate to the Democratic State Convention and in 1890 was elected to the United States House of Representatives at the age of thirty. Re-elected in 1892, he declined to be a candidate in 1894 but sought bigger game, a seat in the Senate. The legislature failed to elect him, but he did not drop from sight. Recognizing the power of the press he went to work for the

[29]

Omaha *World-Herald* as editor-in-chief, from which vantage ground he could present his views on the issues of the day.

W. J. Bryan had lots of bounce. A defeat was only a challenge and that challenge came in 1896 when the vanguard of the Democratic party gathered to nominate a presidential candidate.

> "The scene was at Chicago some twenty years ago,
> The west was all excited, as older people know,
> And silver was the issue and like a roaring tide
> Was rising on the border and sweeping far and wide."

Bryan, age thirty-six, was a delegate from Nebraska and he and Mrs. Bryan took a room in a modest hotel since the family finances were low. Though he already had a wide reputation for his masterful and persuasive oratory, he was hardly looked upon as presidential timber. During the depression years just ending he had been lured by Populist doctrine, though he avoided joining that party. The prominent Populist leader, Ignatius Donnelly, had said of Bryan: "We put him to school and he wound up by stealing the schoolbooks." The free silver issue especially intrigued him and he had spoken on that question to western audiences. What he needed in Chicago was a chance to make the speech that he had rehearsed so many times.

> "But back upon the benches, unknown to fame there sat
> A young man with a lemon, the 'Boy from the river Platte,'
> Who softly sucked the acid and blew the seeds away—
> And destiny and glory sat on his lips that day."

The big moment came when he was invited to close the debate on a resolution, the adoption of which would have repudiated free silver and endorsed Cleveland's stand on the money question. Bryan faced his audience with self-assurance and a smile on his lips, well aware of the power that was his. Even before he had uttered a word the assembled throng quieted down to hear what this young man had to say. Speaking with great deliberation he drove home his message with anvil-ringing harmony. He timed his words and sentences perfectly, placing the accent where it had the best effect.

> "With modesty and calmness he faced the famous scene,
> His form was tall and stalwart, his eye was bright and keen,
> His voice like the thunder rang out upon the sky
> And stirred that great convention as some brave battle-cry."

The Democratic party had found a new leader. As Harry Thurston Peck describes the scene:

"Twenty thousand men and women went mad with an irresistible enthusiasm. The orator had met their mood to the very full. He had found magic words for the feeling which they had been unable to express. And so he had played at will upon their very heart-strings, until the full tide of their emotion was let loose in one tempestuous roar of passion, which seemed to have no end."

In his speech Bryan did not attempt to debate the free silver question. As he put it: "Not to discuss, not to debate, but to enter upon the judgment already rendered by the plain people." It was a call to arms. His closing words have often been repeated, in fact few other of his many utterances can be recalled.

"Having behind us the producing masses of this nation and the world, supported by the commercial interests, the laboring interests and the toilers everywhere, we will answer their demand for a gold standard by saying to them: 'You shall not press down upon the brow of labor this crown of thorns, you shall not crucify mankind upon a cross of gold.' "

If a vote had been taken at this moment Bryan would probably have been nominated by acclamation. As it turned out, he received the necessary two-thirds on the fifth ballot. The "Boy Orator from the Platte" did it with his lethal weapon, his voice. For many years he was destined to hold the party in the hollow of his hand. Never in our previous political history did a candidate make so vigorous a campaign as did Bryan in 1896 but to no avail. The fat campaign chest of the Republican party proved more effective than the crusading efforts of Bryan. Subsequent efforts in 1900 and 1908 met with similar results. These races, however, seem an anti-climax to that of 1896.

William Jennings Bryan was a product of the Middlewest. Born in Salem, Illinois, March 19, 1860, to Silas and Marian Jennings Bryan, he received his early education in the public schools and Whipple Academy in Jacksonville. He graduated from Illinois College in 1881 and went on to study law for two years at Union College in Chicago, graduating there in 1883. While in college he exercised his oratorical skill by participating with marked success in public debates. He practiced law in Jacksonville until moving to Lincoln. Three years prior to moving west he married Mary Baird, daughter of a merchant in a nearby town. She is described as a woman of "unusual mind," and proved to be a great help to him in his many undertakings.

Following his defeat in 1896 Bryan continued his leadership of the Democratic party. His services were much in demand on the lecture platform, especially at chautauquas. When the Spanish-American War broke out he offered his services in any capacity the President might desire. After some delay he was permitted to raise the third regiment of Nebraska volunteer infantry and was appointed its colonel by Governor Silas Holcomb. He published a newspaper, *The Commoner*, from 1901 to 1923, and through this organ kept his views before the people. His efforts in behalf of Woodrow Wilson in 1912 were rewarded by his appointment to the post of Secretary of State, which office he held from 1913 to 1915.

> "The cause it was triumphant, and Wilson felt so glad
> He brought to Billy Bryan the biggest plum he had
> And asked the noted leader to sit upon his right
> And help him in the battle with privilege and might."

Bryan could not go along with President Wilson on the position we should take relative to World War I and resigned from the Cabinet.

> "At last when war-clouds gathered and conscience and belief
> Would not permit him longer to travel with his chief,
> He shook his head in sadness, but calm as man could be,
> And faced the roaring breakers—and jumped into the sea."

It is foolhardy to attempt to do justice to Bryan's career in a few pages but a short appraisal may stimulate further study of this leader of the common man. As everyone knows, his voice was his greatest asset. He was hardly a great thinker. His speeches rendered by anyone else fell flat. But the manner in which he spoke seemed to hold his audiences in a spell. Though not a demagogue, he had the power of one, at least momentarily. Bryan held to certain principles and was never known to compromise his beliefs. Only a few days before his death he matched words with the great Clarence Darrow, steadfastly witnessing to his faith in fundamentalism. The Bible was the source of much of his thinking and he quoted from it frequently. In fact, Bryan might have served a better purpose as an evangelist than a politician. After his three "burials" as a presidential candidate, he did give more time to religious matters. In the final issue of *The Commoner*, April, 1923, he says:

"During the last few years I have given considerable space in *The Commoner* to discussion of religious questions. I have felt it my duty to do this in order that my readers might be fully informed as to the subjects which I was discussing. My Bible Talks now reach a very considerable percentage of the American people, being published in papers with a combined circulation of some four millions."

William Jennings Bryan was, indeed, a champion of causes. For thirty-five years his voice rang out in legislative halls, political conventions, pulpits, and from lecture platforms. In political campaigns he seemed inexhaustible. Eighteen thousand miles were covered in 1896 alone. Not since Henry Clay had a candidate been so vigorous. He kept his poise and remained physically and mentally alert as he pleaded his case for the "toiling masses." Bryan used simple language, easily understood by the common folk. Always the fighter, he spoke out boldly for equal rights, popular government, prohibition, an income tax, child labor laws, and reform in currency and banking. From first to last he fought hard for laws on both the state and national levels to curb the trusts. J. S. Bassett, the historian, says of him:

"In courage and honesty, in wise mastery of a political convention, he has not been surpassed in our political history. It was something like irony that he fought better when fighting for another than when fighting for himself."

Small wonder that one of two statues of Nebraskans in the rotunda of our National Capitol is that of William Jennings Bryan.

WILLA SIBERT CATHER

Writer Extraordinary

DECEMBER 7, 1873 · APRIL 24, 1947

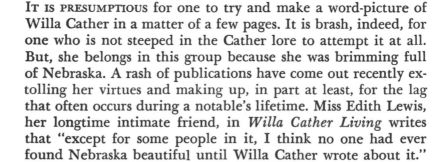

IT IS PRESUMPTIOUS for one to try and make a word-picture of Willa Cather in a matter of a few pages. It is brash, indeed, for one who is not steeped in the Cather lore to attempt it at all. But, she belongs in this group because she was brimming full of Nebraska. A rash of publications have come out recently extolling her virtues and making up, in part at least, for the lag that often occurs during a notable's lifetime. Miss Edith Lewis, her longtime intimate friend, in *Willa Cather Living* writes that "except for some people in it, I think no one had ever found Nebraska beautiful until Willa Cather wrote about it." And, one might add, if more people read her books, that beauty would be appreciated more than it is. Miss Cather had a terrific memory. She came to the state at the age of nine and apparently forgot nothing that happened of her experiences during her impressionable years.

[34]

CATHER, WRITER EXTRAORDINARY

The critic, Victor Haas, makes this comment:

"We Nebraskans do not begin to be vocal enough in our admiration of Willa Cather. An accident of geography made her a Virginian by birth but she was all Nebraskan. I never see the statue of William Jennings Bryan in Lincoln that I do not think he is usurping the place that rightfully belongs to Willa Sibert Cather."

A statue of Willa Cather might be more attractive, and cause less bickering, than that of the Great Commoner, but there is ample space for both. The former, like Jefferson, was facile with the pen, the latter, like Patrick Henry, long on oratory. Poor Bryan can do nothing about it but, undoubtedly, if he could, would graciously step aside and give the pedestal to the Great Lady. Perhaps the recent books and articles will revive an interest in her works and bring the honor which is her due. Mildred Bennett's *The World of Willa Cather*, certainly, should be read by every Nebraskan, old and young.

Miss Cather wrote about the old days, her experiences on the Nebraska frontier. She reached back into the pages of history and allowed her imagination to roam. She wrote of contemporary events with less interest and fervor. She resented the encroachment of the machine age with its destruction of the frontier landscape. The coming of the automobile, bringing improved highways, bothered her no end. She loved horses and looked upon the motor car as an imposter, destroying a way of life sacred to her. This resentment toward change remained with her all through life. Her rebellious nature and aloofness stood in the way of adding new friends, but seemed to draw her closer to the old circle. Old age worried her and sickness was thought of as something disgraceful. As she grew older she was more and more the recluse and stayed away from her early haunts the last fifteen years of her life. Then, too, she found it easier to write of Nebraska from a distance.

Willa was born near Winchester, Virginia, December 7, 1873, of Anglo-Irish ancestry. Her parents were Charles F. and Mary Virginia Boak Cather. The Civil War had caused a rift in the Cather family since Grandfather William espoused the Union cause. The breach seems to have been at least partially healed largely through the efforts of Willa's mother, a charming woman and a loyal southerner. Charles Cather's brother, George, had settled 16 miles from Red Cloud in 1873 shortly after his marriage to the accomplished Frances Smith, graduate of Mount Holyoke Female Seminary. Grandfather and Grandmother Cather visited them in 1874–75 and later, 1877, moved there themselves. It seems that reasons of health was a strong factor in their decision as several in the Cather family had died of tuberculosis because of the humid climate of Virginia. Grandmother Boak also joined them. Charles and Virginia Cather and their children arrived in April, 1883, and took up residence with Grandfather Cather in the Catherton community. The family was hardly settled until Willa's father sold out and moved to Red Cloud where he opened a loan, abstract and insurance office. Along with them came Grandmother Boak and the dull-witted hired girl, Margie, whom they had brought with them from Virginia. In her writings Miss Cather seems to have found a place for all her associates and acquaintances regardless of their station in life, including Margie, Annie the Bohemian immigrant girl, and the beautiful young wife of former governor Silas Garber.

Here in Red Cloud, Willa grew to womanhood. The Cather family lived in a rented house much too small for the growing family. She was the oldest of the seven children. Willa had a deciding voice in many household decisions. Her father was a gentle sort and she was very devoted to him. Her mother, meticulous about her appearance, behaved in the southern tradition to the point that some of the neighbors thought her "uppity." No question but she was a positive woman with a strong will who had the last word as far as most of the family was concerned. However, Willa seems to have had a double-dose of independent spirit and did about as she pleased. She maneuvered a room of her own where she could take refuge with her books and papers. Here in her little niche she built air castles and escaped much of the humdrum of household duties.

Red Cloud was a thriving county seat town of approximately 2,500 people when the ten-year old Willa arrived. It had grown from a handful of settlers in a span of thirteen years. Rail connections were excellent and a heterogeneous mixture of nationalities made this the end of the line. Czechs, Germans, Scandinavians, Russians, French and native Americans were thrown together, all hopeful of improving their lot. These people were not the crude characters often associated with pioneer life. Many, like the Cathers, were cultered, and had much to contribute for the good of the community. Willa recognized this fact and made the most of it. Though her formal education was somewhat erratic, she did graduate, with a class of three, from Red Cloud High School in 1890, giving an oration as was the custom. Her real education was obtained in other ways. She had learned to read from Grandma Boak while in Virginia and her love for literature and history never slackened. Many important people stopped in Red Cloud since it was on the main line of the Burlington and Missouri railroad. Theatrical troupes also appeared at the local opera house. Willa loved the drama and music and availed herself of every opportunity to attend plays and concerts. She helped with school publications in high school and later at the University of Nebraska, showing considerable talent in the journalistic field. As a youngster Willa gave readings and acted in hometown plays. There was always something of the actress in her. Her interests were many and at one time even medical science intrigued her to the point where she had notions of becoming a doctor. But, when she began to see herself in print while attending the University, she gave up the idea.

One hardly connects Miss Cather with sports, but while living in Pittsburgh she raced electric cars on her bicycle. She liked to take hikes and go on picnics and excursions. Willa probably did not interest herself in spectator sports as did Louise Pound, but football evidently caught her fancy, at least for a moment. Frederick Ware in his booklet on *Fifty Years of Football* at the University of Nebraska comments:

"But romance was there, and two co-ed classmates found it. Willa Cather and Dorothy Canfield, daughter of the chancellor, collaborated on a football fiction piece that won the Literary club's first prize and appeared in the university magazine, the *Sombrero*, in 1895."

That was the year Willa graduated with the degree, Bachelor of Arts. She was probably lucky to get a degree for she took little interest in some of the "requirements," especially mathematics. Then, too, she often clashed with members of the English faculty on policies. One of her essays was printed in the *Nebraska State Journal* and later one of her professors helped her to get employment with that paper as a drama critic. Here she had an opportunity to meet some famous writers as well as add something toward the costs of her college education. However, Willa did not work her way through the University as sometimes claimed.

Because of the irregularity of her education in Red Cloud, Willa had to spend a year in the preparatory school at the University before being admitted to freshman standing. She liked to pick her courses, and, since she had made up her mind to be a writer, could see no reason to "waste" time with non-essentials. Her independence, or stubbornness asserted itself at every turn. Some thought her odd or eccentric. She certainly was different. But, she knew what she wanted. Her dress, manners, and tastes were quite unconventional. She could express great warmth for those she loved but made no effort to disguise her feelings for those whom she disliked. While attending the University, Willa made friends with some of the leading families but remained aloof from the usual social life. But she was a top "fan" when it came to operas, concerts, and plays, spending more money than her purse could afford. She was, also, an easy "touch" for her actress friends who were down on their luck.

The half-year following her graduation, spent at home while waiting for a job to "pop," was boring to her and nerve-racking to everyone else around her. When an offer came from *Home Monthly* in Pittsburgh, it eased the pressure in the Cather home. Later she became telegraph editor and dramatic critic on the *Daily Leader*. Tiring of newspaper work she taught English and Latin at Allegheny, Pennsylvania, High School, and used her spare time to write verse and short stories, which were accepted by various magazines. Between 1906 and 1912 Miss Cather served as managing editor for *McClure's Magazine*, one of the muckraking periodicals. Though Miss Cather was no "muckraker," she did become acquainted with many leading literary figures. Living in New York City enabled her to attend the best concerts and plays, something she had always longed to do. During vacations she traveled in Europe and America, with occasional visits back home. Following her stint with *McClure's*, Willa proceeded to grind out her works in an ever steady stream. David E. Scherman and Rosemarie Redlick in *Literary America* say:

"Few American writers have equalled Willa Sibert Cather in understanding the violent clash that occurred in America when the gentle, hopeful, immigrants from the Old World struck the rigorous, inhospitable prairies of the New. To her, it was an eternal preoccupation, and with it she fashioned the greatest of her retrospective novels, *O! Pioneer!* and *My Antonia,* and with little difficulty transposed it to fit the life of a cultured French priest set

[38]

down in a primitive New Mexico desert (*Death Comes for the Archbishop*) and a seventeenth-century French court and his retinue exiled on the icy cliffs of new Quebec (*Shadows on the Rock*)."

Two books on contemporary events, *One of Ours,* and *The Professor's House* were not considered very highly by Willa, yet the former won the Pulitzer Prize in 1922. *Shadows on the Rock* won her the Prix Femina Americaine in 1931. In 1938 she was elected to the American Academy of Arts and Letters, won a Mark Twain award and in 1944 received a gold medal from the National Institute of Arts and Letters. Honorary degrees were conferred upon her by eight universities, including Nebraska and Creighton. Her interest in Catholic subjects and her admiration for that religion has led many to believe she joined the Catholic church. Actually, Willa was an Episcopalian having been confirmed in 1922 by the pioneer bishop, George A. Beecher, and remained a member of that church until her death on April 24, 1947.

Miss Cather had high regard for those who did a job well, whether it be the composing of a musical number, writing a book, or building a piece of furniture. She ridiculed the prevailing superficiality of the times, especially as found among women in joining clubs and taking up nonsensical hobbies, fads, and fancies. The 1920's must have been a nauseating decade to her. She deplored the fact that young people, by their own brazen admission, went to college to get a "soft spot" so they wouldn't have to work like the "old man." These standardized, money-grabbing, "respectable folk" got a low rating in her fiction.

When Sinclair Lewis received the Nobel Prize in Literature in 1930 he said the award should have gone to Miss Cather. He rated her one of the greatest American novelists and declared that "no one has so preserved our frontier ranging from the Nebraska Lutherans to the Quebec padres as she has." Scherman and Redlick make this appraisal:

"Cather went her own way adhering to no school, romantic or naturalist. She believed in the 'unfurnished novel' and painstakingly excluded all but the essentials, which she set down in sparse but invariable luminous style."

Some people consider *A Lost Lady* her best work. Miss Cather sold the film rights to this book for a probable $10,000. She did not see the picture, though the premiere was held in

Red Cloud early in 1925. Her friends thought it an accurate picture of the Garbers. Release of a picture with the same title in the 1930's was very different from the book. This caused Miss Cather to withhold any further sales to the movie industry and she even went so far as to state in her will that "none of her books may ever be dramatized, filmed, broadcast or televised or used in any other medium now in existence or discoverable in the future."

BERLIN GUY CHAMBERLIN

All-American

JANUARY 16, 1894

THE TIME WAS Saturday afternoon, October 23, 1915. Sports fans gathered in the railroad stations all over Nebraska. Big news was coming over the wires. Even the fair sex sensed the tenseness of the moment. With "tantalizing deliberation" came the announcement: "Notre Dame 6, Nebraska 0." This was miserable news. It just couldn't happen to Coach Jumbo Steihm's Cornhuskers. The "Roller" hadn't lost a game since 1912. The sounders clattered again "On the first play . . . of the second quarter . . . Chamberlin . . . ran 20 yards . . . around end . . . to score . . . Corey kicked goal . . . Nebraska 7, Notre Dame 6." This was more like it. On the trains that chugged across the prairies conductors and brakemen passed through the coaches keeping the passengers informed. In the larger towns special hookups clicked the news into halls, barber shops and billiard parlors.

The Sunday papers of October 24th blazed headlines on the Steihm Roller's victory over the great Notre Dame and explained in detail how it happened. More than 8,000 had witnessed the dramatic spectacle and thousands more got the news by wire. All fans were eager to read of "Chamberlin, the Champ's cunning, mad dashes; of his guilful conduct that had rendered worse than useless the notes of Scout Knute Rockne." Chamberlin scored two touchdowns and threw a pass for the third in beating the Fighting Irish. The Notre Dame coach, Jess Harper, consoled Rockne: "But don't take it too hard, Knute. If I'd scouted him it'd probably been the same. That fellow's a demon. Strong's a dozen men and fast as a sprinter. When those long legs start to pound you might know what's comin' but it don't do any good. . . . And what's most important, he won't give up. That big body and crafty mind just won't quit."

Jumbo Steihm was, without question, one of the finest football coaches that ever operated in the Middlewest. His five-year stretch at Nebraska saw the Cornhuskers (or Steihm Rollers) win 35 games, tie three and lose only two. Five titles in five campaigns were wrapped up in the Missouri Valley Conference. A big cog in the Steihm Roller of 1914 and 1915 was Guy Chamberlin. Born near Blue Springs, Nebraska, January 16, 1894, he was one of six children, four boys and two girls. Guy grew into a rugged lad and was a star on the high school football team. His father owned 2,000 acres of land and needed him at home, but sensing the value of higher education, encouraged him to go to college. Nebraska Wesleyan University was his choice and for two years he displayed his football talents so well that he earned All-Nebraska rating as a halfback both years. He was also on the track team.

Such prowess could not go unnoticed. He was induced to switch to the state university where recognition came fast. Because of the freshman rule Chamberlin had to be content with the yearlings his initial year, serving as captain of the team. As a member of the varsity for two years his record is unparalleled in Cornhusker history. The "Champ" scored nine touchdowns in 1914. "Hula-hipping his way through opposing lines, slashing around the ends,—knees high—and possessing a potent stiff arm, Chamberlin was the most feared, the most talked of ball carrier in the Midlands." He seemed to be able to do everything well. Playing offensive back and defensive end he was a terror to Nebraska's opponents. His left-handed passes were feared by all. He was awarded All-Missouri Valley back, All-Western back and in 1915 Walter Eckersall and the United Press selected him for an end position ·on their All-American team—Nebraska's first.

After college Chamberlin taught science and coached athletics in Lexington, Nebraska, High School. World War I ended his teaching career. He enlisted in the army and was commissioned a second lieutenant in the field artillery at Camp Zachary Taylor and later was transferred to the Fort Sill school of fire. Still later he instructed in the 48th field artillery at Camp Kearney, California, and from February to September, 1919, was an athletic director at the same place. After muster-out he lost no time in donning football togs again. That fall he played with Jim Thorpe's Canton Bulldogs, a team that went undefeated and won the world's professional championship.

Though professional football was cutting its teeth in those days yet Chamberlin's feats on the gridiron were heralded by the sports writers. The next two seasons found him playing with the Chicago Bears, a team going undefeated and winning two world's titles. In 1922 and 1923 he was player-coach with the Canton Bulldogs, going undefeated and hanging up two more world's championships. Winning championships had become a habit. Cleveland bought the Bulldogs and Chamberlin coached and played for the new owners. Here he met his first defeat in professional football though still winning the pennant. He still thinks a "fluke" beat them. They were battling the Philadelphia Yellowjackets and were behind with two minutes left to play—according to the scoreboard. The ball was on the opponent's 20 yard line in the Bulldogs' possession. A touchdown would have meant victory. Just then a substitute came in to report that only eleven seconds remained. It was not enough. Chamberlin says that he is certain they could have scored had the scoreboard been correct. His last two years, 1925 and 1926, were spent with the Yellowjackets as a player-coach and he brought them two world's championships. During his football career, both collegiate and professional, he participated in approximately 160 games. In an eleven year stretch his team lost only two games and went undefeated in nine of those years.

Steve Owen, coach of the New York Giants' football team for 20 years, in his book, *My Kind of Football*, has picked an all-time, all-professional football team. Chamberlin is given an end position. He calls Guy "the shrewdest opportunist I have ever seen." Owen should know for Chamberlin says: "We have played Owen's team six different times and never lost to him." George Halas, coach and owner of the Chicago Bears, has also picked him on his all-time, all-professional team. Frederick Ware, former sports writer for the *Omaha World-Herald*, states that "Nebraska has had other players qualified to keep him company, but the time played, coupled with his greatness, seems to make him the symbol of the finest and grandest in Cornhusker football. . . . Significant must be this fact: Members of teams long before and long after those of '14 and '15 call him 'The Champ'." His last appearance in football gear was in a charity game at the University in 1930.

Anything written about Chamberlin's career aside from football may appear as anti-climax. Though football remains his chief hobby he has led a busy life in other ways. After a stint as a salesman for various organizations around Cleveland, 1927–1932, he settled down to the life of a farmer and stockman at Blue Springs. Here he helped his father manage his land and six sets of buildings. The elder Chamberlin lost around $50,000 during the depression years but came through much better than many others. Between 1945 and 1950 Guy operated a Ford tractor agency and recently took over a district managership for the National Federation of Independent Business. He has been active as a speaker and likes to meet groups of young men to discuss with them their athletic activities as affecting their future careers. Chamberlin married Lucille Lees, January 3, 1919, in San Diego, California, while still in service. He has a daughter, Patricia Ann, the wife of a career diplomat, Robert Sherwood.

Not long ago I spent a pleasant evening visiting with Guy Chamberlin. As he replayed his athletic career for me I could not help but think how soon we forget those who have given so many of us so many thrills on the athletic field. He is a fine example for young Nebraskans, a competitor who never knew when to quit. As Walt Dobbins, Sports editor of the *Lincoln Journal* says: "In Cornhusker football history he is the greatest of them all."

WILLIAM FREDERICK CODY

Plainsman

FEBRUARY 26, 1846 · JANUARY 10, 1917

FEW MEN HAVE HAD as many escapades as William F. Cody without coming to a tragic end. But this romantic figure of the plains, better known as Buffalo Bill, seems to have carried a lucky charm. He lived dangerously and died a natural death at the age of nearly seventy-one. Of course many of the wild tales concerning his exploits as an Indian fighter, army scout, buffalo hunter, and showman are figments of the imagination of writers and old-timers. However, there is enough of the real Cody to satisfy the adventurous spirit in most of us.

His career was regional, national, and international, but he kicked up enough Nebraska dust to warrant a claim to him as our very own. Probably, many worried mothers have wished that such a character had never lived, for nearly every boy has tried to emulate Buffalo Bill by staging his own wild west show. Merchants, however, have welcomed such a dashing figure, for he has stimulated the sale of cowboy regalia, Indian suits, and

[45]

other paraphernalia reminiscent of the Old West. He was the Hopalong Cassidy of the frontier days.

Born in Scott County, Iowa, in 1846, young Bill went with his parents to Kansas at the age of seven. The family settled near the present site of Leavenworth, a town the elder Cody helped to lay out. But settling never became a habit with the future Buffalo Bill. He found himself in the thick of a "heated and bitter" political fracas where shooting irons were freely used. This was "Bloody Kansas" where slavocrats and abolitionists were slugging it out for mastery of a new territory. Bill's father fell a victim, in 1857, of exposure while hiding out from his pro-slavery enemies. His mother operated a respected inn on Salt Creek until her death in 1861. But even before she passed away Bill Cody was on his own. At the age of eleven he had killed his first Indian and a year later hired out to the celebrated freighting firm of Russell, Majors, and Waddell. In their employ his frontier education progressed rapidly. He became acquainted with every military fort and trading post west of the Missouri. A favorite with plainsmen and soldiers, his services were in great demand. He learned to handle horses expertly and was a crack shot with a rifle.

When the Pony Express went into operation, young Cody was employed as a rider. In one instance he covered 320 miles in less than twenty-two consecutive hours of riding. The coming of the overland telegraph ended this enterprise. Between 1863 and 1865 he served as a scout against the Indians for the 7th Kansas cavalry. Following the Civil War he was hired by Shoemaker, Miller and Company, builders of the Kansas Pacific railroad, to supply their workers with buffalo meat for a monthly consideration of $500. In 18 months he killed 4,280 buffaloes and earned himself the title of Buffalo Bill.

Cody re-entered the army in the spring of 1868 and was made chief of scouts by General Phil Sheridan. His operations in this capacity included service with the 5th U.S. Cavalry against the Sioux and Cheyennes and the Canadian river expedition of 1868–69. He continued in the role of a scout until 1872, headquartering at Fort McPherson near North Platte, Nebraska. While located here he took his only fling at politics and was elected to the Nebraska House of Representatives where he served one term. Sitting in a law-maker's seat was too dull a life for Buffalo Bill. He craved excitement in the wide open spaces. His next experience was acting as a guide for the hunting expedition of the Russian Grand Duke Alexis. He piloted the party safely, and returning loaded with game, Cody was presented with a scarf pin, studded with precious stones, by the Grand Duke along with other gifts.

Buffalo Bill got his first taste for show business in 1872, though it was to be several years before he put his own show on the road. The play, "Buffalo Bill, the King of the Border Men," by E. Z. C. Judson, better known as Ned Buntline, was being produced successfully in New York. Cody went to see it and was delighted with the performance. "He was persuaded to go upon the stage and be introduced to the audience, which received him with a great ovation. The result was that Buffalo Bill was violently attracted to stage life and wanted to be an actor." Judson, sensing the financial possibilities of personal appearances by the famed plainsman, proceeded to utilize his services. "The Scout of the Plains" included Cody, Texas Jack Omohundro, and a band of "Indians" from the streets of Chicago. A revision of the play, "Scouts of the Plain," added Wild Bill Hickok to the cast. New York crowds were enthusiastic and Cody acquired a stage presence.

But Buffalo Bill's show business had to wait awhile. When the Sioux War started in 1876, he joined the 5th U. S. Cavalry and was soon in the thick of it. In the battle of Indian Creek he engaged in a hand-to-hand fight with the Cheyenne chief, Yellow Hand, sending him to the Happy Hunting Ground. With peace brought to the plains Cody again turned his attention to the entertainment world. His mind was fixed on a well conceived plan. He set out to "collect Indians, cowboys, scouts, trappers, buffaloes, etc.," and produced the Wild West show for the first time in Omaha on May 17, 1883. It was tabbed "The Wild West, Rocky Mountain and Prairie Exhibition." A free preview had been held earlier in North Platte on July 4, 1882. The Omaha performance drew an attendance of more than 5,000 people. His troupe presented scenes and incidents which, only a few years previously, could have been witnessed in reality.

Buffalo Bill's meteoric rise in show business is credited in large part to Major John M. Burke, his devoted friend and press agent. The writings of the dime novel expert, Prentice Ingraham, also made him a household figure. Invitations came from all parts of the country and the show was off to a successful start. Cody continued to enlarge and improve his exhibition and teamed up with Nate Salisbury, already a successful operator in the theatrical field. The famous scout, however, was a much better showman than a business manager. Had it not been for the financial judgment of Salisbury, the show would have, undoubtedly, folded during this early period. Furthermore, Cody was a heavy drinker, spent money lavishly on his relatives and friends, and was a "sucker" for many outside schemes. It seemed that regardless of how much he made, Bill was always in debt. Through Salisbury's restraining influence the two men succeeded in bringing together a combination never seen before which caught the imagination of large audiences both at home and abroad. Nonagenarian W. H. McDonald of North Platte comments on Cody's financial troubles. "He was always needing money. But don't say he borrowed all the money it took to put on his show from our bank. He borrowed from many sources. He made plenty. But he had no sense about spending it. Twice I had to send money to get Buffalo Bill back from Europe. But he always paid us back."

Following appearances in all parts of the United States, Cody and Salisbury received an invitation in 1887 from the American Exhibition Company, which was setting up a display of products at Earl's Court in London, to produce the Wild West Show there in connection with their exhibit "Yankeries." Had it not been for their show the exhibit would have been a failure. But the British were attracted in great numbers and the royal family, including Queen Victoria, patronized the dazzling event. Two command performances were given for her Highness. Edward, Prince of Wales, who was quite a sportsman, rode the Deadwood stage and Buffalo Bill was presented to the queen. With this royal approval the show was all the rage in England.

The troupe now made a successful tour of France, Spain, Italy, Austria, Germany, and Belgium. Returning to America after barnstorming Europe, the show toured this country with even greater success than before. By this time Cody and Salisbury had built up a fortune of nearly a million dollars each, most of it invested in real estate. Two years later the second successful tour of Europe was made taking the troupe as far south as Rome. But, misfortune struck. "The show's cattle became diseased and all the machinery and animals had to be burned." Lacking ready cash Buffalo Bill wired the McDonald bank for 3,000 pounds sterling to bring the troupe home.

Buffalo Bill's wild west show exploited a phase of American

life fresh in the memories of the people and went far in perpetuating these experiences. At the outset he concentrated on things strictly western, such as Indian dances and battles, broncho busting, steer roping, pony races, stage coach hold ups, and the pony express with the emphasis on riding and shooting. Shortly it was expanded to become the "Congress of Rough Riders of the World." Now it included "Mexicans, German Uhlans, French chasseurs, British lancers, American cavalry, Cossacks, Gauchos, and Arabs." Later circus side shows with "snake charmers, sword swallowers, midgets, giants, mind readers, magicians, fire-eaters, jugglers" and other attractions were added. It is estimated that his Wild West Show performed to six million persons at the Chicago World's Fair in 1893. In 1908 the show was joined with "Pawnee Bill's Far East" and this combination lessened the monetary rewards. After a couple more years the profits became less and less. New types of entertainment had entered the field and Cody and his associates found the competition keen.

Though Buffalo Bill made and lost a fortune he gave America and Europe a full measure of popular entertainment and kept alive the spirit of the West. He was, indeed, a picturesque figure. Every one has seen his picture in western regalia, long snow white hair, goatee and moustache. Those who saw him riding his white charger at the head of the procession got a thrill they never forgot nor have they failed to describe it to their offspring. Movie producers have re-enacted the spectacle in both silent and talking pictures, thus perpetuating these memorable scenes of the last frontier.

Buffalo Bill is probably remembered best for his remarkable marksmanship and his uncanny shooting. He, also, trained others in these skills. Shooting from horseback was his specialty and many of his tricks were unbelievable. Among those associated with him were Johnny Baker, a boy prodigy and Annie Oakley. Annie was not a westerner but a native of Ohio. However, she readily passed as the real article. Though portrayed in the movie, "Annie Get Your Gun," as a root tootin' "bouncy, wise-cracking female" she actually was a "nice quiet little woman," well liked by her fellow performers. Buffalo Bill taught her many tricks. Her reputation with a gun was "so widespread that a punched ticket became known popularly as an 'Annie Oakley' because of its similarity to the appearance of a card which the lady herself had shot." Cody's skill with a gun declined as he grew older, but even in his last "farewell tours" he remained the impressive and colorful figure and captivated his audiences with his dramatic and charming movements. In spite of his travels he found time to marry and raise a family. At the age of 20 he married a lovely lady, Louisa Frederic of St. Louis, who shared with him his successes and reverses.

Cody, at various times, owned considerable land. He and Major Frank North once had a ranch on the Dismal River in the Sandhills. His most famous spread was Scout's Rest Ranch adjacent to North Platte. In his later years he settled on land granted to him in Wyoming, and the town of Cody in that state is named in his honor as well as that of Cody, Nebraska. According to W. H. McDonald, Bill did not drink hard liquor the last nine years of his life. He quotes him as saying: "Oh, in my time I've drunk enough to float a battleship. Yes, two battleships. But since I've quit drinking I feel better. Now when I go out to count the cattle and horses on my Wyoming ranch, I can count 'em."

Though dead since 1917, Buffalo Bill still remains the bold knight of the plains, the picturesque figure of the frontier, the Sir Galahad in shining armor in the minds of present day Americans. He is buried at the top of Lookout Mountain, Colorado. Thousands of vacationers visit his shrine each year. From this spot they can look for endless miles across the plains he loved so well. Nebraskans are proud to claim this colorful personality as one of their favorite sons.

GEORGE EVERT CONDRA

Conservationist

FEBRUARY 2, 1869

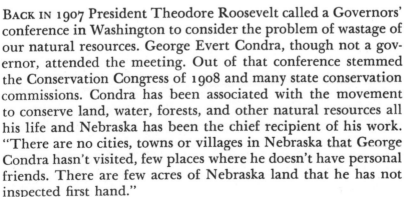

BACK IN 1907 President Theodore Roosevelt called a Governors'
conference in Washington to consider the problem of wastage of
our natural resources. George Evert Condra, though not a governor, attended the meeting. Out of that conference stemmed
the Conservation Congress of 1908 and many state conservation
commissions. Condra has been associated with the movement
to conserve land, water, forests, and other natural resources all
his life and Nebraska has been the chief recipient of his work.
"There are no cities, towns or villages in Nebraska that George
Condra hasn't visited, few places where he doesn't have personal
friends. There are few acres of Nebraska land that he has not
inspected first hand."

"Doc," as he is affectionately called, knows Nebraska and
Nebraskans know him. There is no one who has the intimate

[51]

knowledge of the soil, water, and other resources of the state as he. His efforts to "sell" the people on conservation practices for many years met with much resistance. It has been the practice of Americans to exploit the natural resources of the country, to take rather than give. It is no overstatement to say that George Condra has "given more energy and greater inspiration to the progress of this state" in the field of soil conservation than any other man.

And "Doc" has done his work unselfishly. It is said that he has paid more of his money to the state than he has received in salary. Frugal in his habits, he has conserved his own inheritance and spent wisely. In his later years when he might have led an easier life playing golf, fishing or using the old rocking chair, Condra has kept busy with conservation work. He is not the type to retire as long as he is able to work and his services in demand. Many times he has had opportunities to use his vast knowledge for personal gain but has steadfastly refused to do so. He is concerned with one great motive, to serve the people of his state by advancing sound conservation policies.

Condra is no miracle man. What he has accomplished has been due to straight thinking and hard work. He is a patient man, a plugger, who believes "science isn't something that lies on the pages of textbooks or is bottled up in laboratory test tubes." Science, he believes, is something to practice, to apply to "better the life of the person who puts it into practice—on the farm, in the factory, in the office, or in the kitchen." His department has been a source of valuable information through the years. Surveys made under his direction cover the entire state. He and his companion geologists have made careful explorations, tabulating their findings and registering these in proper form to be available to the public. Their maps are made with precision and clarity. Bulletins describe every new development in understandable language and are furnished to individuals and organizations on request. Condra has always worked on the premise that collected data should be put to use. No significant meetings dealing with conservation practices have been held without "Doc" present to give expert advice. A tireless worker, he boasts of having been sick only once in his entire life. He probably knows more people in Nebraska than any living person.

Whence came this savior of the soil and what has given him his tremendous drive? A look at *Who's Who in America* gives some of the answers—but not all. These facts are mostly a recital of statistics that amaze the reader and do prove that Condra is a man of distinction. Those close to him like Dr. Nels A. Bengston, also of the University of Nebraska, can do it better. But, if one wants an even better picture he should talk with the horny handed farmers who have lived through the same period and know "Doc" intimately.

George Condra was born and grew up on a farm near Seymour, Iowa. He had, as he puts it, "good breeding and good rearing." His father was a pioneer in fighting soil erosion. Too many gullies gutted the farms of Iowa and the elder Condra adopted practices to stop it on his land. Young George learned some practical lessons on how to maintain fertility of the soil and prevent it from washing or blowing away. His mother took time to encourage him in his ambitions and had the good sense to let him "get out and go once in awhile." He grew up to be a big strapping fellow and he played and coached football in the days when there was plenty of body contact.

Condra's first collegiate training was at Western Normal in Shenandoah, Iowa, where he also did some teaching. After a year in the University of Michigan, where he studied chemistry, geology, and paleontology, he entered the University of Nebraska. This was 1892, and now his degrees came in logical sequence: Bachelor of Science, 1896; Master of Arts, 1898; Doctor of Philosophy, 1902. During these years he also headed the science department at Lincoln Normal School, 1892–1896, and held the same post at Lincoln High School, 1896–1902. This would seem sufficient for the most ambitious person but Condra also coached all the sports at Lincoln High and assisted with Cornhusker coaching as well. Then, too, he took time out to marry Hattie M. Davenport, August 13, 1893. What a Man!

"Doc" joined the University of Nebraska faculty in 1902 as an instructor in geography, economics, and geology, rose to a full professorship in 1905, and department head in 1908. He was made director of the conservation division in 1918 and dean in 1929. An ardent sports enthusiast, he played a prominent role in the development of the University's modern athletic department. It was Condra who promoted the Innocents' Society and always took a hand in whipping up enthusiasm at pre-game rallies. He would even "invade" the dressing room between halves to fire up the players, though always insisting on clean sportsmanship. "Doc" was not the kind of professor to spend all his time in the "ivory tower."

The accomplishments of this dynamo of energy since joining the university staff in 1902 have grown steadily each year. Much of his time has been taken up with state surveys, most of which were tied in with the Federal programs. Though he lists himself as a Republican he must have been pleased with much of the New Deal conservation work. He is the author of numerous articles, bulletins, and books on geology, geography and conservation. His geography texts are used widely in the Nebraska public schools. "He has discovered and named more of the geologic formations of Nebraska and adjacent states than any other man." Almost all scientific organizations dealing with land and water include him on their membership rolls, and he has been president of many of these.

Condra has always been a civic-minded person. His community spirit was recognized in 1945 when the Kiwanis award for distinguished service was conferred upon him. He was the recipient of an award from the American Forestry Association in 1951 "for outstanding contributions in the field of public services." He is a 32nd degree Mason and affiliates with the Methodist church. His travels have carried him over most of the world but he is happiest among the friendly people of Nebraska and his work here. It must give "Doc" deep satisfaction to look back over the past half-century and review the progress made in conservation. And, it must give him even greater satisfaction to know that he, personally, played a major role in this program. Many of his ideas, once laughed at as silly notions of an impractical professor, are now accepted as a matter of fact. Soil conservation districts, democratically controlled, now cover the entire state and are supervised by soil engineers trained for the job.

Doc's booming voice in defense of this work will long be remembered throughout the Middlewest. To him efficient use of the soil and water resources mean "conservation of human resources—the values that society in general gains from an agriculture which enhances, rather than devours, its capital foundation." Born on Ground Hog Day, George Evert Condra has been in relentless pursuit for over fifty years of another variety of ground hog, the hog that is a "waster of soil, water and other natural resources upon which life of future generations depends."

EDWARD CREIGHTON

Telegraph Builder

AUGUST 31, 1820 · NOVEMBER 5, 1874

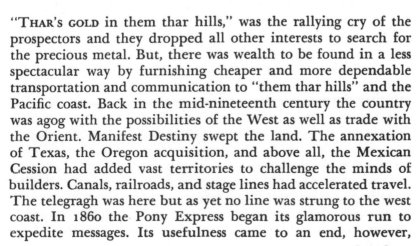

"THAR'S GOLD in them thar hills," was the rallying cry of the prospectors and they dropped all other interests to search for the precious metal. But, there was wealth to be found in a less spectacular way by furnishing cheaper and more dependable transportation and communication to "them thar hills" and the Pacific coast. Back in the mid-nineteenth century the country was agog with the possibilities of the West as well as trade with the Orient. Manifest Destiny swept the land. The annexation of Texas, the Oregon acquisition, and above all, the Mexican Cession had added vast territories to challenge the minds of builders. Canals, railroads, and stage lines had accelerated travel. The telegragh was here but as yet no line was strung to the west coast. In 1860 the Pony Express began its glamorous run to expedite messages. Its usefulness came to an end, however,

[55]

when, under the drive of an Irishman named Edward Creighton, a telegraph wire from the East connected with one from the West near Fort Bridger, Utah, October 24, 1861.

It might appear that stringing a wire across the country should be a relatively simple matter. However, in the Sixties there were many problems to face: raising the capital, effecting an organization, securing the labor, gathering the materials, and the ever-present threat of hostile Indians. It was a job to challenge only those with courage and ability. Edward Creighton was such a man. Already, he had established a reputation as a builder, one willing to take his chances. Perhaps, to him, building an overland telegraph did not pose too many problems. In any event, he set out in characteristic fashion to lay his plans and carry them through.

Edward was born in Licking County, Ohio, August 31, 1820, the son of James and Bridget Hughes Creighton, both Irish immigrants. His father worked in the steel mills of Pittsburgh, Pennsylvania, a young industry then. Young Edward's formal education was limited for he went to work at fourteen to help support the family. These were the days, however, when most young men (and many older ones, too), were gripped with a "get-rich-quick" fever. The Panic of 1837 cast a shadow over the land for several years but young Creighton had no fortune to lose at that time. Perhaps he learned a few lessons on what to avoid in business ventures. State governments, generally, had experienced financial headaches with their enterprises and were now quite willing to leave the transportation and communication business to private management. The corporation came into its own and aided substantially by national, state, and local government loans and subsidies, the building of the West got under way.

Edward Creighton saw the opportunities and determined to be a contractor. He saved some money and took several small jobs. His first big job was the building of a stage highway between Wheeling, Virginia (later West Virginia), and Springfield, Ohio. He, also, built a reputation as a sound and dependable business man. When Samuel F. B. Morse developed his successful telegraph a new field was opened to challenge men like Creighton. He proceeded to build telegraph lines in the middlewest and even in the southwest. He became a "big operator" and was recognized as the country's pioneer in the field. "Blood is thicker than water." Edward was joined by his brother, John

Andrew, and other relatives were associated with him at various times. On his many journeys making surveys for his construction jobs Edward was alert to new possibilities. As his earnings increased he invested more and more funds in the telegraph business and associated himself with men of influence and ability. He was on his way.

Edward was married, October 7, 1856, to Mary Lucretia Wareham of Dayton, Ohio, and their only son died at an early age. The Creightons settled in Omaha in 1860 and from this point carried on a variety of enterprises. Edward had already built most of the Missouri and Western telegraph line extending from St. Louis to Omaha, reaching the latter place in 1859. He was interested in silver and gold mines and cattle raising but his number one desire was to build a telegraph line from the Missouri river to the Pacific. He even had ideas on a line to the Bering Sea to connect with a cable reaching Asia. Creighton, with all his dreams, was a practical fellow. He planned carefully before jumping into a project. He now journeyed to Cleveland and presented his plan for a transcontinental line to J. H. Wade, wealthy financier and leading stockholder in Western Union. This company authorized Creighton to make a preliminary survey.

Returning to Omaha, Creighton took the stage to Salt Lake City where he made a contract with Brigham Young whereby the Mormons were to supply poles for the stretch across the desert. The journey west from this point was made on horseback in the dead of winter. He suffered from exhaustion, hunger, snow-blindness and the severe cold but finally made it to San Francisco. Here he met Wade who had gone out by boat. An agreement was made whereby Creighton would build a line from Julesburg, Colorado, a point already reached by the Missouri and Western Company. This would connect with one to be built by the California State Telegraph Company. The latter, only recently organized, was controlled by Western Union. Congress voted it an annual grant of $40,000 for ten years to help construct and maintain a line.

Actual construction got under way July 4, 1861 and an exciting race developed between Creighton's gang and the California contractors. Two hundred workers were assembled along with a thousand oxen, 400 wagons and an array of tools. The route lay along the Oregon Trail and westbound travelers, freighters, stage coach drivers and passengers, Pony Express riders, and Indians, observed with much interest and curiosity the speedy progress of the line. Bad luck was encountered by both companies, the Indians, especially, giving trouble. Creighton is said to have told the Indians that the messages coming over the wires were revelations of the Great Spirit. Though mystified by the "goings-on" they often cut the wires, so the workers had to double as builders and defenders. Despite Creighton having to cover 1,100 miles to the Californians' 450, his men reached Salt Lake City, October 17, 1861, a week before the western group. The actual joining took place near Fort Bridger, Utah, October 24. The first message from Utah was sent by Edward to his young wife in Omaha and the first from California was sent by Justice Stephen J. Field to President Lincoln. Thus another chapter was written into the saga of western America.

Creighton earned himself a neat sum from this venture but since the telegraph company was low on cash he agreed to take $100,000 worth of stock at eighteen cents on the dollar. This proved to be smart business for he tripled his investment on most of it. Some of his profits were put into overland freighting enterprises which were doing a brisk business at that time. But he was not finished with telegraphy. Creighton served as president and general manager for the company operating between Chicago and Salt Lake City, during which time he built a line from the latter place into Montana. He was, also, attracted to cattle raising and various projects centered in Omaha and helped survey part of the grading for the Union Pacific. Locally, too, he helped organize the First National Bank of Omaha, served as its president, and was one of its principal stockholders. His support helped the bank weather the severe panic of 1873.

Edward Creighton cherished a desire to establish a college where young men might enjoy the educational advantages denied him. He had spent an active life making what was then considered a large fortune. Cut off at the age of fifty-four, he had not yet formulated his plans, but it was well-known that he intended to found this school in Omaha. Edward died November 5, 1874, and his widow two years later. One source says he left a will allowing $100,000 to be used to found a college. Another says he left no will but that Mary Lucretia willed $50,000 to found Creighton University. His brother, John Andrew, who lived until 1907, was executor of the estate and the bulk of it went to him. Having worked in close association with Edward as well as engaging in several ventures himself, such as trading in gold-mining camps, freighting, and the grocery business he, too, built up a sizable fortune. He and his wife gave generously to charitable causes. Creighton University was founded in 1878 and the next year was turned over to the Jesuit Order and incorporated August 14, 1879. Creighton Memorial Hospital, in memory of his wife, and Creighton Medical College resulted from his benefactions. John Andrew Creighton's birthday is still observed as Founder's Day at Creighton University.

Though only fourteen years of Edward Creighton's life was centered in Nebraska, he did more for the welfare of its people than many more publicized figures. Sound in his thinking, he had faith in the future of the state and was daring enough to tackle projects when others hesitated. He must have believed in the saying that "there is no time like the present." The name Creighton will always stand high on the list of builders of the West.

JAMES C. DAHLMAN

Cowboy Mayor

DECEMBER 15, 1856 · JANUARY 21, 1930

JIM DAHLMAN came to Nebraska in 1878 under the name of Jim Murray, having shot a man in Texas. "I shot him, yes," said Dahlman years later when his political foes sought to use this episode against him. "He deserved to be shot. He was my sister's husband; he was no good, and deserted her, and I sent word to him I'd shoot him the first time I saw him. When I left Texas I thought I'd killed him. I changed my name back to Dahlman when I learned I hadn't." In this brother-in-law affair Jim followed an impulse many men have had, but in most cases, have restrained themselves. Frontier justice was speedy and often by-passed the regular court procedures.

Dahlman was always straightforward, plain spoken, and ever loyal to his friends. He never side-stepped an issue or tried to cover up a mistake. He was almost too loyal at times. While

[60]

mayor of Omaha he wrote a letter to J. C. Maybray, a notorious swindler who was operating a confidence game out of that city. In this letter he tipped off Maybray that the "heat was on" and that he had better get out of town. The letter was found among the effects of the swindler and published by Dahlman's political enemies just before the next election. The mayor's supporters urged him to "fix it up some way." Jim said, "I'll just tell them the truth." He called in the reporters. "I wrote the letter of course. I knew Maybray when he and I were cowboys together in western Nebraska and Wyoming. He always seemed like a nice fellow to me. When I heard he was in trouble I thought he ought to know about it. I'd do as much for any friend." The keynote of his campaign was set. "Jim Dahlman sticks by his friends." He was re-elected handily.

That Dahlman's formal education was sketchy there is no doubt, but that fact was of little benefit to his opposition. One prominent Republican declared Dahlman to be "uneducated and illiterate, and didn't know how to write a veto message grammatically." Jim's reply was direct and to the point. "It's true I ain't had much schoolin'. Schools were a long way apart out where I was raised. If I went to school three months in the winter I was lucky. No, I guess I'm not educated. But folks, if you elect me mayor and any ordinance comes up that takes one red cent away from the people unjustly, I'll just write, 'Nothin' doin'.' Any sucker that can't understand that ain't as well educated as I am." The slogan, "Nothin'-doin'-Jim Dahlman" carried him to victory. A newspaper man editorialized that he was ashamed to go to other cities because Omaha had a rowdy cowboy for mayor. Jim replied: "When I first met Theodore Roosevelt he was just a cowboy, too. If this country can have a cowboy for president, Omaha can have a cowboy for mayor."

Jim Dahlman was born in Texas, December 15, 1856. He was twenty-one when he came to Nebraska and hired in at the N-ranch near the present town of Gordon. It didn't take him long to prove his worth in the cattle business. Three years after his arrival he was made foreman of a group of cowpunchers charged with trailing large herds of cattle from Oregon and the Indian Territory to the Dakotas, Montana, and western Nebraska. His next job was that of brand inspector for the Wyoming Stock Association headquarters at Valentine, Nebraska, at that time the end of the Northwestern railroad line. He held this post for two years.

Dahlman was an extrovert with a yen for politics. His first fling came when he tossed his cowboy hat in the ring for sheriff of Dawes county. Elected to this office three times on the Democratic ticket he then served two terms as mayor of Chadron. Here, in true western story tradition, he met the girl of his dreams. Hattie Abbott came from Wellesley College in Massachusetts to teach the children of a wealthy rancher. But, the "spare, wiry" cowpuncher soon ended that career by marrying the cultured young teacher. Undoubtedly, some of this eastern culture influenced the breezy cowboy-politician.

While living in Chadron, Dahlman met with many interesting experiences. One of these was organizing a horse race from Chadron to Chicago during the World's Fair of 1893. Buffalo Bill donated $500 to the purse to be awarded the winners and requested the race end at the site of his Wild West show. Sheriff Dahlman handled the branding iron, marking a small figure 2 on the neck of each horse entered in the race. Nine riders and seventeen horses left Chadron under a haze of dust stirred up by more than 3,000 spectators. Five riders finished the 1,400 miles in less than fourteen days. John Berry came in first and was greeted by Buffalo Bill with a hearty "Well done, John, the race is yours." Such stunts as this not only put Chadron on the map but gave the name of Dahlman greater circulation. His political apprenticeship in northwest Nebraska soon led to wider fields.

Jim was chosen a delegate to the Democratic National Convention in 1892 and again in 1896 when William Jennings Bryan was nominated. In this way he became acquainted with the "right" people and acquired considerable influence in Nebraska Democratic circles. Governor Silas Holcomb appointed him secretary of the state transportation board in 1895. The following year he was made chairman of the Democratic State Committee, holding that post until 1900. Bryan was one of Dahlman's first heroes and he watched with pride as the silver-tongued crusader climbed the political ladder. He conducted Bryan's successful campaign in Nebraska in 1896 and helped keep Bryanism alive for the 1900 campaign.

Dahlman moved to Omaha in 1898 to enter the livestock commission business. That was the year of the Spanish-American War and there was much excitement in Nebraska as elsewhere over the nation. Despite the war Omaha went ahead with its Trans-Mississippi Exposition, plans for which had been laid by Dahlman and others. Jim seemed to "take" to Omaha and that city opened its arms to him. He was offered the position of chief of police but turned down the offer. Apparently he had his sights on bigger plums. After three years with the Union Stockyards he was made manager of the American Commission Company in 1902. Prosperity had returned to Nebraska and Omaha was reaping its share of the profits. It ranked high as a livestock shipping center. Dahlman found it convenient to mix business and politics. For eight years, 1900 to 1908, he served as Democratic national committeeman for Nebraska.

In 1906 a group of Omaha Democrats "tired of always being licked, decided to try something new. They asked Jim Dahlman to run for mayor." Being mayor would mean a financial loss, but the political bug had bitten him hard so Jim, without too much persuasion, agreed. The ex-cowboy had built up quite a following and his popularity carried him to victory through four successive campaigns. Over the country he was known as the "Cowboy Mayor of Omaha" and made a big hit wherever he went. Dahlman was a sound executive and his amiable disposition enabled him to get along with most people. He kept the city's departments working together harmoniously. "He had much to do with getting Omaha a home rule charter; he promoted health work; he worked for an initiative and referendum law; he originated occupation taxes on corporations that brought the city a good deal of money; he helped to reduce electric light rates."

Though a liberal mayor, Dahlman can hardly be called a reformer. Illegal enterprises sometimes operated during his regime and he received much criticism for not "cracking down" more vigorously on the violators. Yet, Dahlman was not accused personally of being a party to corruption. In 1910 he decided to run for governor but the prohibition forces marshalled against him and he was defeated. W. J. Bryan, who wired from India, "All Asia rejoices," when Dahlman was first elected mayor, deserted him in 1910. Jim regarded prohibition as ridiculous and probably thought the whole state was wet like Omaha. Though defeated, he continued to be a power in Democratic politics. In 1920 he was appointed a United States marshal but resigned after a year to again become mayor of Omaha, for the fifth time. Thousands of petition signers had urged him to run and he was elected by a 10,000 majority. In the late Twenties he served still another term.

The young Texas-born cowhand had done right well for himself. His career is interesting, varied, exciting, and successful. He knew how to adjust himself to difficult situations, "to win friends and influence people," and keep up with changing conditions. Colorful in dress, in speech, and in manners, he was without doubt, the best known mayor of any city in the United States. Will Rogers once referred to him as "Omaha's permanent mayor." When Jim Dahlman died January 21, 1930, he was broke. "Omaha funeral directors gave him a lavish funeral, free. Seventy-five thousand people passed by his body as it lay in state at the city hall. Funds were raised to pay his debts and to guarantee Mrs. Dahlman continued possession of the small Dahlman home." His friends did not forget.

MARION IRVING EISENHART

Homemaker

MAY 8, 1883

------◦◦◦◦------

OFTEN OVERLOOKED in the category of Builders is the mother and housewife. We do, on occasion, heap praise on the homemaker and accept her as a necessary part of our "way of life." We know full well that she has had a vital part in our advancing civilization and that without her gentle influence life could not be beautiful. She is referred to as the cornerstone of our moral edifice, as an inspiration to her children and the balance wheel of the home. "What is home without a mother?" Men, rated as successes, respond to the plaudits of their fellow-citizens with: "All that I am and all that I expect to be I owe to my mother." The most wonderful word in the English language is the word "mother." Today, when a drive is on for a worthy cause it is the women who organize and pitch in to put it over. The P. T. A. would fold quickly were it not for the steadying support of the mothers. The men come primarily to drink coffee or because their wives have "twisted" their arms. The women "hew the wood and carry the water." Yet, when medals are passed around they are left holding dust mops, skillets or diapers. In selecting a group of representative Nebraskans it would show a lack of sportsmanship to ignore the mother and housewife.

It may be pointed out that Nebraska women today enjoy unlimited advantages and are blessed with many labor-saving gadgets, especially since the birth of R. E. A. They even handle most of the money. One might argue that they "wear the pants" and rate "top dog" around the home. If so, it is a recent development. It was not always so. Throughout most of our state's history their lot has been an unenviable one. Actually, pioneer women worked harder and displayed more real courage than the men—with a minimum of complaint. The frontier woman was more than a cook, dishwasher, laundry maid, milker of cows, chicken raiser, gardener, dressmaker and maker of beds. She was, also, nurse, "doctor," teacher, spiritual adviser, correspondent, "blues chaser," play supervisor and co-disciplinarian. The "Old Man" carried the title of boss but his wife was prime minister. Seldom did he exude with praise of her efforts. Not that he was unappreciative but he just never got around to it. Neither did he extend himself to ease her lonely life, the routine of which must have been boring indeed. There were many exceptions, however, where "Pa" directed all his energy to providing an easier and happier life for his "woman."

Out in McCook, Nebraska, today lives the gray-haired widow of a Nebraska pioneer banker and the daughter of an early settler from New York state, Mrs. George G. Eisenhart. She is the mother of fifteen children, eleven sons and four daughters. Nine sons and two daughters are now living. Not only did she rear a large family but spent six years of her early life as a school teacher. Her sons and daughters are successful in their chosen careers and living testimonials to this grand lady's superb guidance. Eight of her sons attended the University of Nebraska and were members of the same fraternity. The ninth son was graduated from Kearney State Teachers College. Seven of her sons were in service in World War II, two advancing to colonelcies in the Air Corps. One daughter is principal of East Ward School in McCook and the other the wife of a colonel in the Air Corps and now stationed in the Pentagon in Washing-

EISENHART, HOMEMAKER

ton. Several occupations and professions are included in the repertoire of Mrs. Eisenhart's children including banking, insurance, law, teaching, soil conservation, business and the military. One of her sons is a graduate of West Point Military Academy. All of her children keep her informed regularly about their varied activities. It must bring to her a "grand and glorious feeling" when she surveys the fruits of her labors. They are greatly devoted to their charming mother and highly appreciative of what she has done for them. It all proves that a well managed home in a democratic society will produce fine citizens.

Marion Irving Herman was born in Saratoga Springs, New York, May 8, 1883, and was not quite five years old when she arrived in Hayes County, in southwestern Nebraska, with her parents in 1888. She was of German descent on her father's side and English and Holland Dutch on her mother's. Marion was typical of many children on the frontier and being the eldest child spent much of her time outdoors with her father. She learned how to make herself useful on the farm and developed a spirit of self-reliance. She started to school at the age of seven in a one-room schoolhouse where a three-month term was held each year. There was a stationary bench along each side of the room, a stove in the center and a homemade teacher's table at one end. There was no classification of the pupils by grades. They took whatever the teacher had to offer. Mrs. Eisenhart writes that "she absorbed everything like a blotter except 'figgers' and they never did get through." Perhaps that mattered little since later she married a man who was adept at "figgers." Undoubtedly, her parents supplemented her formal education with "home work" since she made rapid progress in the learning processes.

Educational facilities were not the best in Hayes County at that time and Marion's mother decided to send her back to New York where there were better schools and a more cultured environment. At the age of eleven she made the trip east and lived with an aunt in Saratoga County for six years. There she attended Ballston Spa High School and received social advantages that added to her stature culturally. After being graduated in 1900 Marion returned to Nebraska to rejoin the family, get re-acquainted and adjust herself to the community. Since she had decided to try her hand at teaching it was deemed advisable that she visit a country school for awhile and observe the practices there and "learn the customs." She began teaching the next fall. Marion taught three years in Hayes County rural schools and three years in Culbertson in Hitchcock County. Each summer she would attend summer school to keep up with the new methods. "These were true pioneer days in life and in school affairs," says Mrs. Eisenhart in retrospect, "and the many interesting things would about fill a book." She states further that "the self-discipline of the lonely years on the prairie and the training of young children helped much in later years." Little did she realize at the time that a much greater teaching assignment awaited her in her own household.

While teaching in Culbertson she became acquainted with George G. Eisenhart, a young banker. Their marriage ended one teaching career and started another. The story of Marion Eisenhart from this point is that of a busy housewife and wonderful mother—and one might add, grandmother. As the children began to arrive the problems of organization and management grew apace. Six sons were born before a daughter appeared on the scene. This in itself could have been a problem except that the Eisenhart boys were taught to perform many household chores. It was a well organized family each member knowing his assignments and the time and place to perform them. Each child had his place at the table, each a hook on which to hang his clothes. Regularity became a habit and the older children assisted the younger ones. Not that there were no quarrels or grumbling, for the best regulated families have their moments of discord. But there was a maximum of teamwork and generally the "organization" functioned smoothly with a high batting average for each member of the team. Mrs. Eisenhart comments: "It just took hard work, faith and perseverance. You just never let up for a single day when you have a family." Undoubtedly many prayers were uttered along the way for the Eisenharts are God-fearing people. Mrs. Eisenhart claims no magic formula. It was just a matter of each one doing his job and doing it well.

This mother was typical of mothers of the early 20th century. She cooked, sewed, mended, baked, cleaned and put out big washings with not too much outside help. Living in town she escaped some of the drudgery of the farm but still had more than her share of household cares. George Eisenhart was a devoted husband and father and a man of even temperament. He and his wife "never interfered or overstepped one another's orders." In fact, it seems the whole family had a complete understanding of their mutual problems. The father took a keen interest in the activities of the children and saw to it that they had wholesome recreation. He was not especially fond of rugged forms of diversion himself but did not let that fact interfere with the boys' fun. He often took them on camping trips, roughing it like the rest. On Sundays the family (or as many as could pile into the car with the extra jump seats) would go for a drive after an appetizing dinner prepared by the mother. She relates: "We were a family in which the father just loved all of us. The boys had implicit faith in their father—in his goodness." This faith was, likewise, shared by the patrons of his bank and his neighbors. Farmers and business men often sought his advice on their many problems recognizing his real worth as a sound economic adviser.

Mrs. Eisenhart apparently was the "top kick" in the family. She was firm with the children and when necessary knew how to apply the "little green switch" though this was seldom necessary. However, she was fair and never showed partiality to one child over another. Early in life they learned the meaning of "sanctity of contracts," that promises are made to be kept. Hence, the Eisenhart children developed a sense of responsibility, each carrying his share of the load. They knew the full meaning of the Biblical charge: "Honour thy father and thy mother." Tragedy has invaded the life of Marion Eisenhart. Three of her children died at an early age with diphtheria a disease that now is seldom fatal. A fourth died with a throat infection. There were accidents, too, for it is hard to "ride herd" on such a large brood. Luckily none of these were fatal but nonetheless they added a few more gray hairs to the worried mother. The passing of her husband required adjustments in her life and during World War II she must have had many anxious moments with so many of her sons in the service. But this plucky woman seemed able to withstand troubles and face up to realities with more than ordinary courage. She found the best remedy for heartaches was work and she seems never to have lacked for things to do.

Though family relationships kept the Eisenharts busily occupied, nevertheless they found time for their many friends and for community activities. Marion Eisenhart's careful budgeting of her time enabled her to participate in many organizations. She served on the Library Board, was three times matron of the

Order of Eastern Star, helped with the work of the Woman's Club and is a faithful member of the Presbyterian Church. The family gave generous financial support to many worthy causes. She and her husband were followers of athletic events. This interest stemmed from the fact that their boys were athletically minded, some of them participating in football, basketball and track. They always extended themselves to attend all the games in which their sons participated. Their interest was equally keen in activities in which their talented daughters participated. The Eisenhart children must be grateful indeed that they have had parents who gave them the opportunity and encouragement to make for themselves successful careers. Few have enjoyed such a bountiful heritage.

In spite of her advancing years Marion Eisenhart is still a very alert woman. She presents a beautiful picture with her gray hair worn in pompadour style, her vibrant face set off with dark, penetrating eyes and a well groomed and trimly dressed figure. It must be satisfying to look back upon a life well spent. Her greatest reward is seeing her children leading useful and well adjusted lives. She keeps up on the current developments and still gets a "kick" out of a University of Nebraska football game. Whether she agrees that children are "cheaper by the dozen" doesn't matter. What really matters is that she is, as a recent article in the *World-Herald* puts it, a "Mother Extraordinary." Marion Irving Eisenhart has indeed been a homemaker deluxe and is a shining representative of Nebraska motherhood. In fact she has made motherhood an art.

EDWARD JOSEPH FLANAGAN

Humanitarian

JULY 13, 1886 · MAY 15, 1948

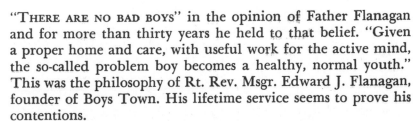

"THERE ARE NO BAD BOYS" in the opinion of Father Flanagan and for more than thirty years he held to that belief. "Given a proper home and care, with useful work for the active mind, the so-called problem boy becomes a healthy, normal youth." This was the philosophy of Rt. Rev. Msgr. Edward J. Flanagan, founder of Boys Town. His lifetime service seems to prove his contentions.

Few people in this country, or even in foreign lands have not heard of Boys Town located ten miles west of Omaha on U. S. highways No. 6 and No. 30. The film, "Boys Town," made in 1938, starring Spencer Tracy as Father Flanagan and Mickey Rooney as the typical bad boy, spotlighted attention on the "city of little men" and brought it much moral and financial support. A second film, "Men of Boys Town," released in 1941, strengthened this support. Here was a place where democracy was being practiced, not just preached, a place where boys of every race, class, and creed could gather on a common level.

Boys Town did not just happen. It was not an accident. Rather, it was the fulfillment of a dream, a carefully preconceived plan in the mind of a lowly priest who wanted to do something tangible for underprivileged youth. His ideas did not crystallize overnight but shaped up after he spent three years trying to help older men, "the down-and-outers who drifted into Omaha." He established his "Workingman's Hotel" where derelicts could secure food and shelter and supported it through gifts of money, food and labor, which he personally solicited.

"Thousands of destitute men were guests of the young priest. As many as 500 were given food and a bed in a single night. Those who could, paid a dime, but none were turned away because he could not pay. Almost every type of person was helped. Generally, however, the men were a tough lot, including gamblers, dope addicts, and drunkards, as well as men out of work. Some of these men Father Flanagan was able to rehabilitate, but he was not satisfied with his modest success. He studied those men as they came and went. He asked them questions about their youth. Almost without exception he found that these human derelicts had been homeless, neglected boys who had started in their present ways of living because no one was interested in them in the early years when their habit patterns were formed. It was then that Father Flanagan decided to quit trying to straighten the gnarled oak and go after the young sapling."

These three years, 1914–1917, determined the course that Father Flanagan would follow the rest of his life.

The young priest was only 31 when he started Boys Town in a two-story house at 25th and Dodge streets in Omaha, December 12, 1917, with five boys and $90 borrowed money. Soon overcrowded, he moved to the German-American Club rooms on South 13th Street, June 1, 1918. Facilities here proved inadequate so his next step was to purchase an 160-acre farm ten miles west of Omaha, the present site, which was occupied on October 17, 1921.

The founder of Boys Town was born July 13, 1886, in County Roscommon, Ireland. He had the advantages of a good home and sound training. His early education was received in Ireland and he came to the United States in 1904 and soon became a naturalized citizen. His collegiate work was done at Mt. St. Mary's College, Emmetsburg, Maryland, where he received a Bachelor of Arts degree in 1906 and the Master of Arts degree in 1908. This college conferred an honorary Doctor of Laws degree on him in 1938. Similar honorary degrees were granted him by St. Benedict's College, Atchinson, Kansas, in 1939, and by Creighton University in 1941. Flanagan studied at St. Joseph's Seminary in Dunwoodie, New York, 1906–1907, Gregorian University in Rome, Italy, 1907–1908, and at Jesuit University, Innsbruck, Austria, 1909–1912. Here, indeed, was a man well-schooled to render intelligent service to humanity.

Ordained a priest on July 26, 1912, in Innsbruck, Austria, his first charge was at O'Neill, Nebraska. He served here until March, 1913, after which he became an assistant pastor at St. Patrick's Church in Omaha for three years. A similar assignment was held at St. Philomena's Church in the same city for more than a year. During these years of apprenticeship Father Flanagan familiarized himself with local conditions and laid plans for his future career. Establishing an institution such as Boys Town was not easy, and during those early years Father Flanagan had to labor hard and patiently to secure public support. But he was not one to give up easily and he mounted each obstacle that arose.

A survey of Boys Town as of 1950 shows how far Father Flanagan had gone in the realization of his dreams. There are 1,000 acres of land. The grade school section includes a school building, gymnasium, dining hall, four apartment buildings, chapel, dental and medical center. The high school section includes a modern school building, trade school building, dining hall, and recreation center, auditorium, administration and welfare building, 25 cottages to house 20 boys each, reception center, visitors' center and a field house. The farm section includes a dairy barn, pasteurizing shed, cannery, slaughter house, root cellar, farm residences, six miscellaneous storage barns, 600 acres farmed, which include a 60-acre vegetable garden. The Dowd Memorial Chapel, a gift of the late Mary A. Dowd of New York City, was built in 1940 and is, undoubtedly, the most beautiful structure in Boys Town.

Boys are accepted between the ages of 10 and 16. More than 6,000 have called Boys Town their home. One-thousand Boys Town graduates saw service in World War II, forty of whom gave their lives for their country. The present enrollment exceeds 750 and facilities are being made available for 1,000. "Boys Town is a complete community in itself—with its own boy mayor, four boy councilmen, and 17 boy commissioners." Each boy has an opportunity for self-expression, may learn a trade, participate in wholesome recreation and extra-curricular activities and follow the religion of his choice. Boys Town is supported entirely by voluntary contributions from people who believe in Father Flanagan's philosophy that "there is no such thing as a bad boy." Never has Boys Town received any support from a church; local, state or federal agency; or a community chest.

Father Flanagan, through his work at Boys Town, became an international figure and was honored in many ways by groups and individuals for his humanitarianism. He was honored by Pope Pius XI on October 23, 1937, by being elevated to Domestic Prelate with the title of Right Reverend Monsignor. He was given the Humanitarian Award by Variety Clubs of America in 1939; selected National Chaplain of American War Dads, 1945; named to a national panel for the study of juvenile delinquency problems by U. S. Attorney General Clark, 1946; appointed a member of the Naval Civilian Committee by Secretary of the Navy Forrestal, 1947; and was a member of the executive board of the Covered Wagon Council of Boy Scouts of America as well as a representative of the National Council, B. S. A. At the invitation of General Douglas MacArthur and the U. S. War Department, he made a trip to Japan and Korea in 1947 to study child welfare problems there. He died in Germany in the spring of 1948 while on a similar mission to that country and Austria.

Father Flanagan was ever in demand by organizations both in and outside of Omaha. He helped to establish the Boy Scout movement in Omaha and was president of the Omaha Welfare Board for ten years. But, Boys Town was his first and continuing love. "While the world has widely honored this distinguished humanitarian," he experienced "his greatest satisfaction in the smile of the homeless boy who found comfort and opportunity at Boys Town." The fame of Boys Town "has been spread by the movies, in song, over the radio, on the stage, from the platform, in magazines and newspapers, and by thousands of people who visit Boys Town each year." Its famed choir and stellar athletic teams have traveled thousands of miles performing before large audiences. More recently television has brought the work of this institution into countless homes. What better monument than "a city of little men" could there be to the memory of the Irish-American priest who set out on that cold December day in 1917 to establish a home for the "abandoned, neglected and underprivileged boys of every race, color and creed."

HAROLD GIFFORD

Ophthalmologist

OCTOBER 18, 1858 · NOVEMBER 28, 1929

———◆◉◆———

PHYSICIANS SELDOM make the headlines. They do their work quietly and without fanfare. There is no thundering applause from the grandstand. Often they are charged with exacting unwarranted fees from their patients. People forget the free service rendered the poor and old, unpaid bills wiped from their books from time to time. Some doctors, like those in other professions, are greedy and do hike their fees. But, these are the exceptions. Most physicians do not take the oath of Hippocrates lightly. These medical scientists who put in long hours and are subject to call at all hours deserve more recognition. Though dedicated to the healing arts, these doctors are among our best citizens, giving freely of their time and money for worthy causes.

Such a man was Dr. Harold Gifford who will be long remembered as Omaha's greatest eye, ear, nose, and throat specialist.

His eminence in his profession was national and international. But, Omaha knew him, too, "as the public spirited citizen who by word and by deed was interested in better things for his city, in a better life for its citizens." He has been applauded as "by far the most indispensable citizen with which Omaha has ever been blessed." The Omaha American Legion Post No. 1 chose him as the "Most Valuable Citizen" for 1927. This civic service citation epitomizes the public contributions of the great doctor.

"Builder of the health and citizenship of Omaha's children; author and sponsor of far-seeing designs for the city's orderly and beautiful growth; donor of places of beauty for the recreation and inspiration of all the city's people; lover of nature and of its wild life, whose energy and foresight have preserved them for the city's future generations; open-handed giver to public causes and private charity; fearless exponent of constructive plans for the greater Omaha of the future. As the resident of greater Omaha, who by 40 years of devotion to these ends culminating during the year 1927, has made the greatest contribution to the city of disinterested and unselfish service, unassociated with his vocation and personal interests."

This award was especially significant in that he was considered a pacifist and a socialist, neither palatable to the Legion. In accepting the honor, Dr. Gifford took the opportunity to explain his philosophy.

"I had been informed in a rather mysterious manner that something like this was to happen. I was surprised, as I had believed the American Legion was against pacifists and socialists. But if you can believe that a pacifist is one who abhors war and its evils, and studies it in all its phases to the end that some day war may be abolished forever and ever, and if you can believe that a socialist is one who studies conditions with an eye to alleviating injustice, then I am both. And I am very happy at receiving this honor."

Harold Gifford was born in Milwaukee, Wisconsin, October 18, 1858. His father was a horticulturist and young Harold, though greatly interested in that field, chose to study to be a doctor of medicine. He was graduated at Cornell University with a Bachelor of Science degree in 1879 and received his M.D. degree from the University of Michigan in 1882. He did postgraduate work in New York and in later years went abroad and studied in Vienna, Erlangen, and Zurich. Gifford began practice as an ophthalmic and aural surgeon in Omaha in 1886. He soon established a reputation in his specialized field as a doctor of distinction. The young physician was selected to head the Eye, Ear, Nose, and Throat Department of the Nebraska Methodist Hospital and was a charter member of its medical staff serving from 1891 until his death. He was, from 1903 to 1925, professor of ophthalmology at the University of Nebraska College of Medicine and was given emeritus status when he retired.

Into his offices in the Medical Arts building "there flowed day in and day out, probably as complete a cross-section of Omaha city life as in any one place in Omaha." Rich and poor alike sat in the waiting line and took their turns and no one was turned away for lack of funds to pay his fee. Once Gifford decided to give his attention only to children but the demands were so persistent from people of all ages that he had to abandon his plans. However, during the latter part of his career he did devote himself primarily to surgery of the eye.

Dr. Gifford kept posted on the latest developments in his field. He traveled much in foreign lands for he was filled with a tireless scientific curiosity and wanted to learn everything he could in his specialty. In Vienna it is said that his name was mentioned with greater feeling and respect than any other American physician. In the fields of pure laboratory research, clinical observation, therapeutics, and ophthalmic surgery he had no peer. He wrote for various ophthalmological journals in the United States, England and Germany, making his findings available to other physicians. Between 1897 and 1915 Gifford edited the *Ophthalmic Record*. There was nothing selfish about this famous surgeon. He gladly shared his knowledge with his colleagues. Memberships were held in the American Medical Association, Nebraska State Medical Association, of which he was president in 1907, American Academy of Ophthalmology and Oto-Laryngology, and American College of Surgeons. The University of Michigan conferred the honorary Master of Arts degree on him in 1912, and the University of Nebraska the Doctor of Laws in 1920. He was decorated by the Serbian government in gratitude for his gifts to the Serbian Relief Commission during World War I.

In the field of civic enterprise Dr. Gifford left an indelible impression. He was the inspiration of River Drive and gave tracts of land in and south of the city for parks and reserves, including the land on which the Boy Scout camp is located. A student of political and social problems, a lover of the great outdoors, and a botanist of note, Dr. Gifford lived a rich and full life. He was a member of the Omaha Club, Fontenelle Forest Association, and Alpha Delta Phi fraternity. He married an Omaha girl, Mary Louise Millard, in Geneva, Switzerland, in 1890. Four children were born to this union. The atmosphere of the Gifford home was typically American.

The passing of Doctor Gifford on November 28, 1929, was mourned by all citizens, young and old, for so many had come to rely on his services. But, his works followed after him for he had passed on his skills to an untold number of doctors and nurses. Dr. C. W. M. Poynter, Dean of the University of Nebraska College of Medicine said of him:

"Some people called him a socialist. To me he seemed more like a fundamental Thomas Jefferson Democrat in that he recognized no stratification of society. He saw only one fundamental right, and that was based on individual ability."

ALFRED MAXIMILIAN GRUENTHER

Ace Planner

MARCH 3, 1899

LAST AUGUST, 1953, Alfred Maximilian Gruenther, native Nebraskan, was made Boss of the North Atlantic Treaty Organization, popularly known as NATO. This is the organization
that is charged with building up the defenses of Western Europe against threats of communism. He was the personal choice
of President Eisenhower and his appointment came as no surprise, for these two men have been closely associated as a team
since before we became involved in World War II. As someone
has said: "They operate better together than they do sepa-
rately" whether it be planning and executing military strategy
or as partners at the bridge table. Both are experts in each field.

Gruenther has spent very little time in his native state, nevertheless, Nebraska has a better claim to him than any other state.
Most of his life has been spent moving from place to place on

army assignments. Since his work has been more on the quiet side, that of a staff officer, his name until recently has not been prominently in the headlines except, perhaps, when directing or participating in a national contract bridge tournament. Many Nebraskans are unaware that they have such a distinguished and accomplished representative.

Though the public has not been too familiar with his importance he has been long regarded with great esteem in military circles for Gruenther is the "soldier's soldier," the brains behind many successful campaigns. General Eisenhower was quick to recognize his worth and has utilized his services since 1941. A top German general once said that "a clever and industrious" officer belongs on the General Staff. Al Gruenther measures up to these qualifications. He is described as "incredibly industrious," and judging by the success of his planning as a staff officer he must be unusually clever—or lucky. He is probably the hardest working soldier in the whole American Army, putting in extremely long days and often working several hours in the evenings. Yet, he manages to thrive on this routine, keeps an even temper at all times and his affable smile is almost as contagious as the famous Eisenhower grin.

Major General Tasker H. Bliss wrote in 1917 when he was Chief of Staff of the Army that "untiring industry, helpfulness, self-sacrifice and self-effacement are the foundation stones of efficient staff services." He further stated that "tact, good temper, forbearance, alertness, willingness to accept responsibility, reserve, good judgment, and straight thinking, not to mention personal valor, would be the conspicuous characteristics of the perfect staff officer." A long measuring stick but this "fast-stepping, smiling little chap of 152 pounds," Al Gruenther, seems to possess all of these qualities. He comes close to being "Mr. Perfection," himself. His success at public relations is attested by the fact that the press corps, the Pentagon, Congress, and European leaders find so little to criticize in his actions. When an army officer is so highly esteemed personally he must be good. Gruenther knows his facts and they know he is not talking out of an empty head.

The NATO Commander believes in good "housekeeping" in the armed forces. In the Army "he is known as a sort of human IBM machine." Careful organization, well-trained personnel, imagination and above all, plain hard work, are in his book the keys to an efficient operation. He wants his associates to know that it is a privilege to work for the Government. Gruenther will not tolerate "sloppy or incomplete work" in his subordinates and, by example, sets the pace he expects to be followed. He recognizes the power of public opinion in a democracy, that the military arm cannot be projected beyond the wishes of the policy makers. Hence, he knows there is always a selling job to do—and Gruenther is a "great salesman." An effective speaker with a prodigious memory that stems from a memory course he took in prep school, he knows how to present his ideas in a clear-cut and understandable way. He knows how to meet the press, a congressional committee or any other group in a calm, straightforward and relaxed manner. He knows, too, how to leave unsaid those things that might not, from the standpoint of defense, be for the best interest of our country. His sense of humor enlivens his talks and though his audiences may not understand all he says as he reels off yards of statistics, they do feel that he knows what he is talking about. Gruenther years ago, sensing that an officer would be called upon frequently to speak in public, took an evening course in public speaking. Continuous self-improvement has always been a factor in his life. He has the knack of anticipating needs.

All these words of praise raises the question: "How did he get this way?" An old proverb gives much of the answer: "As the twig is bent." Al Gruenther was bent early. Parental influence was strong, kind and effective. His father, Christian Gruenther, was of German extraction; his mother, Mary Shea, was Irish. Alfred Maximilian, eldest son in a large family, was born in the little town of Platte Center, Nebraska, on March 3, 1899. Chris Gruenther, ably assisted by his wife Mary, published the local weekly, the *Platte Center Signal*. As a young man he had worked as a farm hand and saved enough money to attend college one year. He was a Democrat in politics and came to play an active role in the affairs of the party. In addition to his publishing he was a land auctioneer and for nineteen years was Clerk of the District Court. Though his duties necessitated his being absent frequently, he kept close supervision over his household for Chris Gruenther believed in discipline. Young Al, who was a "chip off the old block" except in physique, had his chores cut out for him and hence grew up in the atmosphere of a well-regulated home. But he had time to play and baseball was his favorite game. His father often entered into the sport with the boys and he taught Al how to play "checkers" because he thought it was good mental exercise.

Al Gruenther's education was well planned. Chris seemed to want him to do the things that he had been denied. Since the family was Catholic in religion the children were sent to the local St. Joseph's School for their grade school education. Like most boys his age Al was up to certain mischievous tricks and he seemed to be more clever than his classmates. He made fairly good grades without over-working his brain cells. Having finished grade school at thirteen Al was sent to St. Thomas Military Academy, a Catholic preparatory school in St. Paul, Minnesota. His father paid his expenses but he sold magazines and worked at odd jobs for his spending money. At this point the future general had no particular desire to follow a military career. In fact he showed signs of pacifism when he editorialized in the *Signal* while on vacation and during a short absence of his parents, that all the officers were concerned about was war and getting promotions for themselves. He wrote that it would be more sensible to put the money in hospitals and libraries. His father straightened him out when he returned home. This attitude was hardly good policy for one with a German name and a war on in Europe. Al thought seriously about studying for the priesthood and also toyed with the idea of being a doctor. His record at St. Thomas was not particularly brilliant though he did excel in mathematics and chemistry. His father checked his progress methodically and required him to write a newsletter home each week.

When half-way through prep school young Gruenther began, with encouragement from his father, to give serious thought to a military career. Chris, taking no chances on Al "flubbing" the entrance examinations to West Point, sent him to Washington for a refresher course. Senator Gilbert Hitchcock made the appointment to the Academy and Al passed his tests with ease. Now that he knew what he wanted the young cadet applied himself with vigor. Due to the War a speed-up program was in effect and he was graduated in November 1918, placing fourth in his class. At West Point Al Gruenther was considered a "grind" and some of his classmates thought him a bit "mousy." It is doubtful if many would have predicted for him more than ordinary success.

Graduating too late for participation in World War I, and following a tour of the European battle areas, Gruenther was assigned to Fort Knox, Kentucky, as an instructor in field artillery and chemical warfare. He also taught other subjects including military history, courtesy and mess management. While here he fell in love with and married Grace Crum of Jeffersonville, Indiana, who was working as a secretary at the Fort. About a year later the young lieutenant's father died from injuries sustained in an automobile accident. It was a severe blow to Alfred as the two had been so closely associated together. He was granted a six month's stand at Omaha so that he could help settle up the family affairs, then with his wife and infant son Donald sailed for the Philippines. Gruenther was stationed there for several years during which time their second child, Richard, was born. Both sons are now army career men and, like their illustrious father, graduates of West Point. Things were rather quiet in the Islands during the Twenties. Al had time to play though it is hardly correct to say that he plays. Whether it be tennis or bridge Gruenther plays seriously and he does both well. In 1927 he was assigned to the West Point Military Academy as an instructor in chemistry and electricity. He proved to be a capable teacher and steadily gained more confidence in himself.

Perhaps the game of bridge has affected his career more than even he is aware. Having met with some embarrassment at a social affair because of his ignorance of the game he decided to do something about it. He set to work in dead earnest to become an expert and he did just that. His mathematical mind and terrific memory stood him in well and while at West Point he played in several tournaments and refereed some big matches. He even wrote a rulebook which became a standard text. His services as a bridge referee were in great demand and, it may be added, the fees he received helped materially in furnishing the Gruenther home. Mrs. Gruenther learned the game along with her husband and became an excellent player and the two often played in tournaments as partners.

Army promotions come slowly in peace time. Though he got his first lieutenant's bars in 1919, Gruenther waited until 1935 for a captaincy, proof that he is, indeed, a patient man. It would be tedious to follow all of his assignments from the time he graduated to World War II. While at West Point he was shuttled here and there for short tours of duty. The "Big Deal" came, however, in 1936 when Captain Gruenther was assigned to the Command and General Staff School at Fort Leavenworth,

Kansas. Now he knew he was headed for greener pastures. A year at this post was followed by another at the Academy, then came further training at the Command and General Staff School and the Army War College in Washington. He was made a major in 1940. Promotions now came fast. War had broken out in Europe and we were sitting on a "hot stove." The best brains were in demand and Major Gruenther had such equipment. In September, 1941, he was raised to a lieutenant colonelcy and three months later—the month we entered the "shooting war"—he was made a colonel. How fast can a man rise? Early in 1942 it was Brigadier General Gruenther (temporary).

Up to this time Gruenther had had only one field command, that of the 15th Field Artillery Battalion at Fort Sam Houston, Texas. He had participated in the Louisiana maneuvers where he got some practical field experience. Gruff old General Walter Krueger tried to ruffle him by saying that he had spent "too much time at West Point and too little in the field." Undoubtedly Gruenther felt the same way but probably thought it discourteous of the old walrus to point it out so bluntly.

Events moved swiftly in 1941 and Alfred Maximilian Gruenther was in the thick of the fast-moving drama. That year found him back in Washington serving at General Headquarters on Lieutenant General McNair's staff along with Brigadier General Mark Clark. Gruenther and Clark became good friends and the latter was a close associate of Colonel Dwight D. Eisenhower who had just returned from the Philippines to be Krueger's chief of staff. Krueger now commanded the Third Army. Clark proceeded to recommend Gruenther to be Ike's deputy and strangely enough Krueger heartily approved. Here began an attachment that has never ceased. Eisenhower has since remarked: "It was love at first sight. I was intrigued by the little devil. He always had a joke or a wisecrack, he had all the answers at his fingertips, and he never got tired. His adrenal glands were going like a house afire."

Eisenhower was on his way up and when he was briefed and processed for his European crusade Gruenther was, at Ike's request, made Krueger's chief of staff—but not for long. When Eisenhower arrived in England he sent for Gruenther to serve as deputy to Walter Bedell Smith, his own chief of staff. Though Al left Washington on short notice and without time for briefing he set to work immediately on his assignment. This was none other than that of chief planning officer for "Operation Torch," the North African invasion project. He really sweat on this one but within six weeks the whole plan had been worked out to the minutest detail. The events that followed are known to all. The operation was successful beyond the wildest dreams of those who planned and directed it. Gruenther was awarded the Distinguished Service Medal for his part in planning the invasion and the Legion of Merit for his role in the ensuing campaign.

In the Italian campaigns that followed Gruenther served as Mark Clark's chief of staff with the Fifth Army. Here he continued his fine executive skill as a planning officer coordinating the operations of the various units harmoniously. Later, when the 15th Army Group was formed comprising American, French, British, Italian, Polish and New Zealand forces under Clark's command, he served in the same capacity. This was a job requiring the utmost tact but Gruenther, now raised to major general, carried out his assignment with consummate skill. After the surrender of the Germans he served as deputy commander to General Clark in the American Occupation Zone in Austria. He returned to the United States in 1945 and served first as Head of the National War College, then in 1947 was made Director of the Joint Staff which was working out plans for the unification of the armed forces. In 1949 he held the position of Deputy Chief of Staff for Plans and Combat Operations.

Gruenther now was considered the recognized authority on planning and chief "trouble-shooter." His advice was sought at every turn in working out plans for the defense of Europe. He was constantly in close touch with all important defense agencies such as the State Department, National Security Council and Central Intelligence Agency. As usual, hard work and lots of it was on his daily menu. "Gruenthergram" was added to the Army vocabulary meaning a white slip of paper carrying a question or an order and causing both superiors and subordinates to scurry in every direction. "Gruentherize" was another term that meant asking someone enough questions to squeeze "a question or a situation" to the main essentials. Gruenther's reservoir of up-to-date information resulted in his being given many special tasks. Everyone at the Pentagon made a "work-horse" of him but he did not seem to mind. He made frequent trips to New York to brief Ike on latest developments. Eisenhower was then serving as president of Columbia University. When he left the cloistered life there late in 1950 to become Supreme Commander of NATO forces, he immediately called for Gruenther to be his chief of staff. He commented later: "Al was the service specialist on international affairs" and understood the problems to be faced completely. Now advanced to a lieutenant general, Gruenther was off to Paris in January with a small but capable group of assistants and by early April, Supreme Headquarters, Allied Powers in Europe (SHAPE), was officially in operation near that city. In the administration of SHAPE both Ike and Al agreed that personnel should be kept at minimum requirements and resisted all pressure to "bureaucratize" the organization.

When Ike came home to campaign for the Presidency he would have preferred that Gruenther be made head of NATO. However, the European members felt that a more experienced field officer should be in command and the post went to General Mathew Ridgway. Last year, 1953, on Ridgway's promotion to Chief of Staff of the Army, Ike's man moved up to take the position. Now Al has his first big command post and from all reports is doing a "bang-up" job. Said Ike: "I think he can do just about anything he puts his mind to." And, there is no denying that the Platte Center product has put his mind to many things. Currently, Gruenther is back home doing "public relations" work. He points with pride to the growing strength of NATO and calls it a powerful shield against the communist menace.

There is one field in which Al has little authority—the Gruenther home. "I'm commanding officer around here" says his wife Grace. Early in their married life she found herself being submerged by what seemed to be countless Gruenthers. So, in self defense she organized the "Anti-Gruenther Society" as a bulwark against too much "Gruentherism." With the addition of many in-laws the "Society" has grown in size. It's main objective today is to "keep General Gruenther from assuming that his four stars carry any weight outside the Army," or that a divine halo encircles his brainy head. Grace Gruenther's friends say she is an excellent homemaker despite their nomadic life.

Alfred Maximilian Gruenther has come a long way since his Platte Center days. He is a credit to his native state and Nebraskans should be proud that he decided on a military career. This master planner, who can assemble and digest a mass of facts and map out a sound course of action, may be the salvation of our Country and other democracies in this time of world crisis. The Nation can use more leaders like him.

HOWARD HAROLD HANSON

Composer

OCTOBER 28, 1896

THE EASTMAN SCHOOL OF MUSIC, a department of the University of Rochester in New York, is well known throughout the country. Not so many are aware that the fame of this school is in large part due to the efforts of its director, Nebraska-born Howard Hanson. He took this post back in 1924 on an invitation from George Eastman of kodak fame, and the President of the University of Rochester, Rush Rhees, and has held it ever since. He had gone to that city to conduct his *Nordic Symphony* with the Philharmonic Orchestra and had met these men there. Apparently, they were greatly impressed with the performance of the 27-year old conductor for shortly thereafter he was invited to head the school.

The following year Hanson inaugurated a series of American composers' orchestral concerts. The purpose was to give beginners and amateurs an opportunity to hear their productions and it served as sort of an experimental laboratory for him. From these concerts has developed the annual Eastman School Festival of American Music, an event that has been held every year since 1931. At this yearly affair a variety of music, chamber, choral, symphonic and stage, is presented. Here in an elaborate, moon-faced hall the public 7,000 strong listen, free of charge, to native compositions played by an outstanding orchestra under the baton of Dr. Hanson. Many young composers who, ordinarily, would never have the chance to display their wares are given their big opportunity. Old established composers also put their works on the line. Thus, the people not only hear the new productions but can observe the direction American music is taking. Orchestras all over the country draw heavily from these compositions. Through this device and in many other ways Dr. Hanson is credited with having done more to advance American music than perhaps any other person. He continually seeks to convince conductors that they should play more American music. He tells them that there are many people with the technical skill to express, through their music, the life of the country and that this talent should be warmly supported.

Howard Hanson believes that a composer should be free to express his "artistic conscience" unhampered by theories. This, in his opinion, allows any serious-minded musician to give greater emphasis to his ideas and feelings. An example is that of Roy Harris, an ex truck driver whose *Folk-song Symphony* played by the Rochester Philharmonic in 1940 under Hanson's direction, brought down the house. The audience broke local precedent by shouting approval and continued until the composer took five curtain calls. Harris was not an Eastman product, yet his work was described as the "most notable premiere of the week."

Howard Harold Hanson was born in Wahoo, Nebraska, October 28, 1896. His parents, Hans and Hilma Kristina Eckstrom Hanson, are described as "good Americans, good Swedes, and good Lutherans." This description would fit many of the settlers in and around the little town with the Indian name, Wahoo. Howard recalls that the name "Wahoo" was useful in making up yells for high school football games. He thought Wahoo above average in culture for a town of its size. Here was a good public school and a small Swedish academy-college, naturally called Luther. Howard had the advantages of both, as well as instruction from his mother, who was a musician. At Luther he received not only a sound general education but a "solid musical grounding" giving him the proper start toward a great career. He learned to play the piano and the cello and, apparently, showed no resistance to practicing on these instruments. His "early musical fare," he recalls, "consisted of Swedish folk songs and Lutheran chorales on the one hand and the usual public school music diet of that period on the other. My earliest musical memories are a mixture of *Sweet Adeline, Down by the Old Mill Stream,* Necken's *Polska,* . . . Lutheran chorales, the *Messiah,* and something by Grieg."

When only fifteen, Howard enrolled at the University of Nebraska for further study. His next effort was at the Institute of Musical Art in New York City. While there he was awarded a teaching fellowship to Northwestern University where, in addition to the regular academic subjects, he studied composition, acoustics, and the piano, receiving the Bachelor of Music degree in 1916. During his student days there he taught musical theory and gained valuable experience for his future work. Returning to the Institute of Musical Art, he studied piano under James Friskin and composition under Percy Goetschius. This latter artist urged Hanson to become a composer rather than a concert pianist, a suggestion he accepted. The public had not long to wait for his compositions as he went to work with a vigor characteristic of this young Swede. He, shortly, accepted an offer to teach theory and composition at the College of the Pacific in San Jose, California, and not long after was made Dean of its Conservatory of Fine Arts. His productions began to attract the music world and his score for the *California Forest Play* and a symphonic poem, *Before the Dawn,* won him the *Prix de Rome* in 1921. More important to him, was a fellowship carrying three years residence in Rome with an annual allowance of $2,000, plus the privilege of travel.

These years in the Italian capital were both productive and profitable for the young musician. They were stirring ones, too, on the political front with Mussolini's march on Rome and the attendant changes. But, Italians do not let such things upset their musical activities. Their appreciation for good music was stimulating to the young maestro and the classical atmosphere of Rome added to his educational stature. Here he wrote his *Nordic Symphony,* and *Lux Aeterna,* the premieres of which he conducted in Rome and which were highly applauded. He attracted the attention of Walter Damrosch and was invited by that celebrity to direct the New York Symphony in a first performance of another product of his stay in Rome, *North* and *West*. It is interesting to note that Dr. Hanson credits the North and the West as the two principal sources of his best music—Scandinavia and Western America.

Waving his baton in New York City was only the beginning of a long and successful career as a conductor. Aside from his regular directing in Rochester, he has been a guest conductor in most of the major American cities as well as a number of cities abroad such as Stuttgart, Rome, and Leipzig. At the request of the Italian government in 1930, he directed the Augusteo Orchestra when American compositions were being played for the first time. The following year he was sent by the Oberlaender Trust as a goodwill ambassador to Austria and Germany in an effort to promote a better understanding between this country and German-speaking peoples. Music is said to know no boundaries but politicians and diplomats tend to wreck any international understanding developed through this medium. In spite of the efforts of men like Hanson, Europe was soon to be torn apart by the most destructive war in history.

Though his duties have multiplied since he became head of the school that Kodak built, Dr. Hanson has found time to produce many outstanding works. His most significant one is probably the opera, *Merry Mount,* a delightful, melodious number that had its premiere at the Metropolitan Opera House in New York city in 1934. But, there are others that have received high acclaim from the critics such as *Pan and the Priest,* the *Heroic Elegy, Beat! Beat! Drums!, Romantic Symphony* (the first symphony by an American-born composer to be conducted by the great Arturo Toscanini), *Lament for Beowulf, Pope Marcellus Mass, Hymn for the Pioneers, Exaltation,* and *Symphonic Rhapsody,* in addition to those previously mentioned. A fairly recent production is his *Symphony No. 3.*

While composing and conducting may have brought him greater publicity, training teachers of music is probably his most vital concern. Those who attend the Eastman School of Music are given a most intensive training in both theory and practice. Through his students Hanson's influence is immeasurable. Just as his compositions reflect a frank and youthful vigor suggestive of his Scandinavian background, so, too, does his teaching express an intense and emotional feeling that is contagious to those who come under his instruction. His ever-ready smile of approval to those who do a good job is something to see. His effervescent personality seems to extract the best performance from his students.

It goes without saying that one of such creative mind would be called upon to contribute his learning to many music organizations. He has served as chairman of the Commission on Curricula since 1925 and as head of the Music Teachers National Association for two years. He has served on advisory boards of many musical organizations including the American School of the Air. The National Institute of Arts and Letters made him a member in 1935 and the Royal Academy of Music in Sweden a fellow in 1938. There seems to be no end to the honors heaped upon this prodigy from Wahoo. Many universities have granted him honorary degrees including the University of Nebraska, recognizing the worth of this prodigious conductor, composer, educator, and eminent scholar.

Howard Hanson is tall and lanky and has a rather boyish face touched up with a goatee and topped with straggling straw colored hair. He is stoop-shouldered but not from family cares as he has remained a bachelor all his life. Perhaps this fact has spared him more time for his music activities. At any rate there is no denying the fact that his contributions to the fine arts are excelled by few. "Through his own compositions, through his guest conducting of most of America's great orchestras, through his leadership of the Eastman School of Music, through his work in many musical and music-teaching organizations, this accomplished musician has wielded a tremendous influence in the musical life of our times." Nebraskans can well be proud that he had his beginnings in the grassroots of the Cornhusker state.

GILBERT MONELL HITCHCOCK
Publisher

SEPTEMBER 18, 1859 · FEBRUARY 3, 1934

THE OMAHA WORLD-HERALD monopolizes the newspaper front in Nebraska today. Of this there is no doubt. How much its influence affects its politics is a question for debate. John Gunther believes it to be a vital institution with tremendous power over the lives of the citizens of the state. The founder of this newspaper hardly realized he was establishing an organization that would so profoundly affect the midwestern region.

Gilbert Hitchcock had a well filled life in which he played at least two roles, that of a journalist and a politician. His contributions were solid ones. Born in Omaha, September 18, 1859, he was indeed an example of "Home town boy makes good." Before he was eight years old Nebraska had become the 37th state so the life of Hitchcock parallels the growth of this commonwealth. He came from "good stock." His father Phineas, native of New York, was a lawyer in Nebraska and served one term as U. S. senator. Hence, young Gilbert grew up in a political atmosphere. His early education was acquired in Omaha after which he was sent to Baden Baden, Germany, for further training. Later he entered the University of Michigan where he took a law degree in 1881. He settled down to practice in Omaha, but like so many lawyers who have the political itch, an attorney's office does not satisfy the effervescent nature of an extrovert. After four years Hitchcock bade farewell to law practice and henceforth journalism became his obsession.

In this venture he started from "scratch." In 1885 he founded the *Evening World,* the first issue emerging August 24th. In this initial move he had some associates but gradually purchased their interests. When President Grover Cleveland visited Omaha, October 12, 1887, Mr. Hitchcock went all-out to observe the occasion. He printed the first page of a number of copies of the *Evening World* on satin with pictures of the President, his special car, and notables who accompanied him. Included, also, was a handwritten welcome and stories of Mrs. Cleveland's real estate holdings in Omaha with congratulatory notes from representative ladies of the city. In 1889 he bought out the *Morning Herald,* a Democratic paper dating from 1865, and merged it with the *World* to form the *World-Herald.* Now he had a morning, evening, and Sunday newspaper.

The newspaper business was a touch-and-go business in those days and for several years Hitchcock was beset by financial woes. It required real fortitude to buck the depression years of the 1890's. At the outset the *World-Herald* had only a scattered circulation but steady progress was made. Hitchcock was a persevering young man alert to the public interest with an eye to the future. His father was a Republican and he was nominally one for awhile but more and more assumed an independent position. He engaged a Republican and a Democrat to present the issues, a rather unique approach but one that caught the public fancy. However, Hitchcock left his independent shelf and threw in with the Democrats though, to the end of his career, he displayed an independence of judgment on many issues.

Shortly after the birth of the *World-Herald,* W. J. Bryan spent two terms in Congress and following this was employed by Hitchcock as an editor. Bryan used this outlet to advance the fight for free silver, a low tariff and to attack the abuses of monopolies. The two years with the paper seems to have worked to the advantage of both men, at least for awhile. But the activity of each in Nebraska politics brought a cleavage. The "break" was not sudden nor especially deep but a lasting friendship did not develop for their personalities clashed and they stood apart on many issues. Bryan had been defeated in his efforts to become a United States senator and apparently did not care to see Hitchcock elevated to that post for he prevented his appointment in 1899. Though the *World-Herald* supported Bryan in his several bids for the Presidency, more and more Hitchcock aligned himself with Arthur Mullen and the anti-Bryan crowd. While Bryan parted ways with President Wilson on the war question, Hitchcock, as chairman of the Committee on Foreign Relations, was a staunch supporter of the President during and following World War I.

Under Hitchcock's direction the *World-Herald* became an organ of great influence and steadily expanded its operations. Following an inauspicious beginning (it's original capital was $15,000) the financial worth grew to $50,000, later to $75,000, then $250,000 and finally reached $1,500,000. It supported Democratic policies and candidates in state and national affairs. It followed a pattern of liberalism supporting reforms such as the direct primary, popular election of United States senators, municipal ownership of public utilities, low tariff, banking and currency changes, regulation of trusts, and went all-out in backing Wilson on the League of Nations question. Opposition was made against national prohibition, a stand later upheld in the repeal of the 18th amendment.

Though wrapped up in the political battles from the start, Hitchcock's personal participation in public affairs really started in 1902 when he was elected to the House of Representatives. Defeated for reelection in 1904 he came back and won in 1906, and again in 1908. Here he grew in stature and in 1911 was sent by the legislature to the Senate, being the first Democrat to be sent to Washington from Nebraska in that capacity. He was reelected in 1916, hence his service in the Senate coincided with the reform period of Wilson's first administration, the war years, and post-war reconstruction. His faithful support of the President proved extremely valuable in a time of domestic transition and international chaos. As a member of the Banking and Currency Committee he rendered yeoman service both in the committee and on the Senate floor in putting through the Federal Reserve Banking system. He, likewise, was a valuable member of the Military Affairs Committee and of that of the Philippine

Islands. Legislation was passed giving more local autonomy to the Filipinos though full independence, a platform promise of the Democrats, had to wait until the New Deal days.

The post-war reaction brought defeat to Hitchcock. The "roaring Twenties" saw the Republicans and Big Business having a field day. "Normalcy" Harding, "Cool Cal," and the "Engineer" Hoover were at the helm with solid backing in Congress. The gentle, firm, and persistent publisher from Nebraska went back to the active direction of his publishing business. He had fought a game but losing fight against the forces of Senator Lodge for acceptance of the Treaty of Versailles. He honestly believed that the League promised a new order of world peace. Perhaps, if left to his own political "know-how," he might have compromised on the question but he remained loyal to his Chief to the bitter end. Hence, he lost some of the fame that would have been his had the fight ended successfully.

Though out of Washington, he continued his avid interest in politics. In fact he twice again sought to secure a Senate seat. He was unsuccessful in the 1930 primary against George W. Norris and failed to get an appointment from Governor Charles W. Bryan in 1933 when Senator Howell died. He could hardly have expected favorable consideration from a member of the Bryan family. Hitchcock's career was not especially a dramatic one. He was not one to play to the galleries but he followed a steady day-to-day down to earth policy with his feet firmly planted on solid soil. A study of his journalistic and political career gives one a perspective of the history of Nebraska from the frontier days into the turbulent Thirties of the New Deal. A Jeffersonian Democrat, yet Hitchcock was never allergic to change. He did not pose as a savior of mankind but lent his voice and pen to reform and kept pace with sound progressive movements which he believed would make for a more enlightened and equalitarian democracy.

Gilbert Hitchcock was civic minded and supported worthwhile causes. His interest in the youth is shown by the granting an annual $200 scholarship to a top boy and girl graduate of each of Omaha's high schools, a practice still continued by the *World-Herald*.

He never backed away from a fight and kept up a running battle with Edward Rosewater and his *Omaha Bee*. But his fights were sometimes within his party, yet he stood his ground and acquitted himself in excellent fashion. His perseverance is shown best in his initiating a newspaper and keeping it in continuous operation for nearly fifty years to a greater capitalization and circulation. With his multifold duties he found time for his favorite recreation, golf and travel, as well as for his family. He was married twice. His first wife, Jessie Crounse, died in 1925 leaving two daughters, Margaret, wife of Henry Doorly, and Ruth Hitchcock. He married Martha Wormley in 1927. He passed away in Washington, D. C., the scene of his political battles, February 3, 1934, just as the New Deal was taking shape. It would be interesting to know how far he would have gone with this program. But, "How much history can one man make?" Gilbert Hitchcock had made his share.

EDGAR HOWARD

Country Editor

SEPTEMBER 16, 1858 · JULY 19, 1951

FEW PEOPLE HAVE LIVED as long or full a life as Edgar Howard. This nonagenerian was as picturesque a figure that ever trod on prairie sod. His active career in Nebraska politics and journalism covers nearly sixty-eight years, for he wielded his sharp pen right down to the finish line. He was a county judge, state legislator, lieutenant governor, congressman, and a "wheel horse" in the Democratic party. These bear witness to his aggressiveness in politics. His favorite role, however, was that of a country editor. When in Congress he described himself in the Congressional Directory as "holding contemporaneously with all those official places the higher office of Editor of a country newspaper, and still in that estate."

A featured article in *Time Magazine* while Howard was in Congress had this comment:

"Impartial House observers rate Edgar Howard thus: a fine example of what congressmen were in the last century, plus a pointed ubiquitous sense of humor, an adept at floor strategy, able to transcend House rules of debate by his witty, original methods, thus an insidious protagonist of minority measures. Perhaps he is the greatest 'character' in the House, and the most universally loved congressman."

One, closely associated with him, makes this evaluation: "He was a gifted writer with a distinctive style of expressing his thoughts; educated in the law; an eloquent, entertaining and convincing orator; a student of history with an exceptional memory, and intensely interested in the cause of the 'common man'. It was natural, then, that he should be interested in a political career."

Edgar Howard has been called the "Old Roman," "Patriarch," and in more recent years, the "Sage." He has been characterized as "amiably erratic," "pleasingly unpredictable," "utterly fearless," an "independent thinker," a "commoner," a "humanitarian," a "square shooter," "versatile," "kindly in spirit," "individualistic," and a "natural gambler." He was not one to give up easily. A year before he died he wrote: "For weeks the doctor has tied me in the stable. I am able to look out the window and see the rich pasture, but to give it no more than a yearning look. I have been a good fighter. I may defeat my present illness."

Some have called Howard "eccentric" because of his manner of dress and his habit of wearing his hair long. About two years before he died he ambled into Andy Mlinar's barber shop in Columbus, Nebraska, and got himself a "crew cut." Needless to say that this was news. He wore black or gray clothes with frock coat of the Chesterfield period and a large black or tan hat. Howard and W. J. Bryan were life-long friends but if there was any "aping" of dress or hair style it was W. J. B. and not Edgar who did the aping. A colleague said of him: "He is first of all, 'Edgar Howard,' and the Lord broke the mould after he was fashioned, because no man who ever served in the United States Congress ever retained his individuality—his own distinct personality—more than Edgar Howard—unless it was his life-long friend, George Norris."

Edgar Howard was born in Osceola, Iowa, September 16, 1858. His father was a native of Ohio and his mother was a Virginian, hence Edgar was under both northern and southern influence. His education had its interruptions. Due to his "pre-cociousness," and on recommendation of his teachers, he was transferred from the public school in Glenwood, Iowa, to the Western Collegiate Institute, a private school in the same town. Later he attended Iowa College of Law (later merged with Drake University), but his professors thought he "did too much window-gazing in class a few weeks before commencement" and held up his diploma. A few years later, however, he passed the bar examination in Nebraska and was admitted to the practice of law. Law practice was not particularly appealing to Howard except as it aided him in the journalistic and political fields.

His first job as a "printer's devil" was on the *Weekly Opinion* in Glenwood at the age of fourteen. In Des Moines he worked as a "cub" on the night shift of the *Iowa State Register* where he learned the "case"—handsetting type. Denied a law degree, he became a "tramp printer" and writer, working on papers in a number of large cities. He finally settled down for a full year as city editor of the *Dayton* (Ohio) *Herald*. But, Edgar dreamed of the day he would own and edit a country newspaper and his dream was partly realized in 1883 when he acquired an interest in the *Papillion* (Nebraska) *Times* and became its editor. Three years later he sold out there and established the *Dundy County Democrat* at Benkelman, Nebraska. Here he found himself in an area where the "cowmen" and the "nesters" (homesteaders) were sparring for position and there was a lot of bad blood. Howard did not flinch in stating his opinions and these were none too favorable to the cattle barons. When working at night he kept his Winchester rifle handy. The opposition knew he was an expert marksman and showed him due respect.

After three years at Benkelman, Howard returned to Papil-lion and bought his "first love," the *Times*. The next year he was a delegate to the Democratic State Convention and nomi-nated W. J. Bryan for Congress and helped secure his election. While in Papillion Howard found time to serve four years as county judge and was Bryan's private secretary in Washington for a short time but resigned because he could not live on the salary paid. Howard liked to play poker and it is likely that the Washington crowd was a bit too fast for him. There is a story (told on himself) that a few days before his marriage to Eliza-beth Burtch of Bellevue, Nebraska, in 1884, her uncle gave them $500 as a wedding present. But he made the mistake of giving it to Edgar instead of Elizabeth. Edgar then slipped into

Omaha and lost it in a faro game but kept the news from her until after their marriage. He never lost his love for poker, however, and through the years matched his wits with his colleagues. During his twelve years in Congress he "quit poker cold," not because he feared the "wolves," (so he said), but rather to have time to discharge his duties.

In 1894 Howard was elected a representative to the state legislature and served one term. He was a candidate for Congress in 1900 but was defeated. Late in the same year he bought the *Columbus* (Nebraska) *Weekly Telegram,* though there were five other weeklies being published there at the time. It was here that Edgar Howard was destined to make his reputation. For more than a half-century he operated the *Telegram* and during that period he was always the fearless writer. He plunged into every political campaign that came his way, either to champion another candidate, or as a candidate himself. No man ever "cowed" him in his editorial or political career, by threats of physical violence or financial ruin. He always loved a fight and on many occasions "stuck out his chin" to invite controversy with political opponents. No matter how vitrolic his pen had been some of his most formidable political enemies remained his warmest personal friends. Howard, according to a colleague, considered himself a "free" Democrat, one who reserved the right to take issue with his own party leaders "if they depart from his concepts of true democratic principles." Edgar Howard's "free Democrat" political views were very much in line with those of George W. Norris, "independent Republican."

Howard was elected lieutenant governor in 1916 and served one term. In 1922 he was sent to Congress by the voters of the third district and served there until defeated by Karl Stefan in 1934. This defeat was a disappointment but did not embitter the "Old Roman." He continued to give all-out support to Franklin D. Roosevelt but on his death in 1945 would not go along with Harry S. Truman. He said he could not "in good conscience," support one of the Pendergast gang. Both in and out of Congress Howard fought for a square deal for agriculture, veterans, Indians, organized labor, small businessmen, and home owners. He opposed mixing in the politics of Europe, calling himself a "George Washington Democrat."

The year, 1922, when first elected to Congress, he sold most of his stock in the *Weekly Telegram* to his associates. At their request he retained enough stock so that, as long as he lived, he might be president of the corporation as well as editor of the paper. That same year it was converted into the *Daily Telegram*. Not only through the paper was Howard's influence felt but he was always active in the affairs of his community. He was a Mason (past master), an Elk, member of the Country Club, and the Chamber of Commerce, and an Episcopalian in religion. Always a colorful figure at meetings of the Nebraska Press Association, he was once president of the organization. He made a bid for the lieutenant governor's office in 1936 but failed to get the nomination. In 1938 he was an unsuccessful candidate for Congress. Howard's last active appearance in politics was as a delegate to the Democratic National Convention in 1944.

Howard's colleagues and friends have praised him highly for his humanitarian acts.

"He is 'tender hearted as a child.' He'd give his last 'buck' to a tramp printer or anyone else who didn't know where his next meal was coming from if he was 'on the level.' . . . He has probably found more jobs, in private and public employment, for men and women who needed them than any other man in Nebraska—or even the Federal-State Employment bureau—in the same span of years. Never did he accept a fee for such service . . . He is equally at home in the presence of the president of the Union Pacific railroad company, or president of the United States, both of whom were personal friends, and in the presence of the humblest farmer, laborer or clerk. He recognizes no lines of social distinction."

Senator Norris said of him on the occasion of his 40th year with the *Telegram:*

"Edgar Howard is a man whose heart is always on the right side and whose inclination is to assist his unfortunate brother. His words of wisdom appearing in the many editorials he has written would, of themselves, constitute almost a Bible for human guidance. No one can value or estimate the good that he has done during his forty years of labor. No one knows how many an unfortunate has looked at the shining light which comes from his wisdom and gained renewed courage in the struggle of human life. From him, and such as he, a numberless multitude of our fellow-beings have received new inspiration, new hope, and new courage in the struggle for human existence."

The "Old Roman" passed away, July 19, 1951. Most of his old friends preceded him. But Edgar Howard had many young friends, too. Making friends was his habit. Once he wrote a poem, *For Friendship's Sake*. One verse goes as follows:

"True friends are God's best gifts to earth—
True friendships are the priceless boon.
Let's strive to price them at their worth
Nor lose them from our lives too soon."

WILLIAM MARTIN JEFFERS

Railroad Giant

JANUARY 2, 1876 · MARCH 6, 1953

WHEN YOU THINK of railroads, if you are a Nebraskan, the Union Pacific comes to mind. When you think of the Union Pacific you think of Bill Jeffers. The history of the "U. P." is one of the most colorful sagas in the annals of American railroads and so is the life of William Martin Jeffers. He was the "Pride of North Platte," Nebraska, and the whole territory served by the Union Pacific, for that matter. When this dynamo of human energy was made head of that railroad on October 1, 1937, he said it was a greater thrill "to become president of the Union Pacific than to be elected president of the United States." No doubt he spoke from the heart, for with 47 years of railroading in his blood Bill had reached the top. Seven thousand, five hundred employees and members of their families gathered for a dinner in Omaha on that eventful day to pay "tribute to the first man to become president of the Union Pacific who had no other employer."

This "modern Horatio Alger" proved that truth may be stronger than fiction. From call boy in 1890 to president in 1937 is, indeed, a remarkable achievement. Little wonder that this "man who drank his coffee with the labor gangs and hoisted cap with the lowest ranking employee—who came through the ranks step by step" was idolized by thousands. It could happen only in America. Neither is it strange that the street of his birthplace in North Platte has been changed from "Locust" to "Jeffers" and the humble Irish home was moved to a city park for a museum.

William Martin Jeffers was born in North Platte on January 2, 1876. He was one of nine children of William J. Jeffers, an employee of the Union Pacific shops there. When only 14 he left school to help support the family, and here begins his long, faithful and distinguished career with the "U. P." It would be easy to glamorize the Jeffers' story but that would be unfair to the man. His rise in the "System" was not meteoric, but it was steady. Each rung of the ladder was taken only when he was ready for it. During his first four years he rose from call boy to clerk in the maintenance department, timekeeper, extra-foreman of the steel gang, and telegrapher. This latter job was the pay-off for utilizing his spare time to study telegraphy. That same year, 1894, he married Lena A. Schatz, daughter of a Union Pacific employee. Two years later Jeffers was made a dispatcher and in 1900 was advanced to chief dispatcher. The new century brought more recognition, first trainmaster at Green River, Wyoming, and Denver, then assistant superintendent, and later superintendent of the Wyoming division which in 1911 was extended from Cheyenne to Ogden.

In 1915, at the age of 39, Jeffers was called to Union Pacific headquarters in Omaha and made superintendent of the Nebraska division but shortly was advanced to general superintendent of all divisions. Less than a year later, June 3, 1916, he became general manager of the "U. P." and on July 1, 1917, was made a vice president as well. We were now involved in World War I and the Government "took over" the railroads. Jeffers management "kept 'em rollin' " and his skills were, also, of inestimable value in the post-war reconstruction and reorganization. There were many problems to be worked out in returning the roads to private owners, and Jeffers played an important role in these negotiations.

On October 1, 1928, Jeffers was elected vice president in charge of operations for the entire Union Pacific system with authority over all separate "units." These "properties" were brought together as an integral part of the Union Pacific company with about 10,000 miles of track extending from Omaha and Kansas City on the east to Los Angeles and Portland on the west. This action effected more economical operation and better service to the public. A new position, "Executive Vice President," was created by the Board of Directors in 1932 and Jeffers was given the post. This was merely a prelude to the presidency to which position he was elevated on the retirement of Carl R. Gray in 1937.

The coming of the Great Depression in 1929 taxed the business acumen of management in every field. The railroads in particular took a terrific beating. Rail transportation found itself in a highly competitive circle. Bill Jeffers measured up to requirements of these critical years. He improved public relations, promoted the efficiency of the company's personnel and kept pace with the mechanical developments of a streamlined age. But Jeffers went beyond this. One who has "supped at labor's table" would have been an ingrate, indeed, if he had not acted to maintain satisfactory working conditions for employees. He never forgot the worker in overalls and took pride in the fact he could recall the first names of more than 10,000 "U. P." employees.

Recognizing, long before many others, the possibility of our becoming involved in a second world war, Jeffers began to map a plan with the steps to be taken by the Union Pacific to meet such an emergency. Surveys of equipment likely to be needed were made. Designs for more effective power were completed. Nothing was overlooked in the event of American participation in such a conflict. He pledged the support of the "U. P." to the plane manufacturers and other producers of defense materials.

"Already orders had been placed—for new and more powerful locomotives, thousands of freight cars had been authorized and materials for other thousands had been delivered to the railroad's own car building shops to insure constant and continued employment for its own forces. Large tonnages of heavy steel rails were ordered and when delivered work was started on hundreds of miles of new track installation ... And so, long before war actually came to the United States, the Union Pacific was prepared to carry on its full share of the American railroad slogan to 'keep 'em rolling'."

Bill Jeffers was an "earthy" leader. Through the years he never lost touch with the men in the ranks. The employees who "knew Jeff when" always felt free to walk into his office and discuss their problems. He organized the "Union Pacific Old Timers Club," restricted to those who had served the railroad 20 years and was, of course, a charter member. He, also, formed the "Junior Old Timers Club" for those employed from 5 to 20 years. Through such activity he built and maintained an esprit de corps that kept up the morale of the "U. P." household.

The year 1939 was an eventful one for Omaha—and Bill Jeffers. He brought the premiere of the motion picture "Union Pacific" to the city and took a leading part in organizing the "Golden Spike Days" celebrating the 70th anniversary of the completion of the transcontinental railroad. Omaha put on its old "bib and tucker" and "pulled all the stops" to make it a gala affair. "Jeff" was in his "seventh heaven." Ak-Sar-Ben, the Midwest's outstanding civic organization, honored him the following year with the kingship of the mythical realm of Quivera. No doubt he was a bit embarrassed with the tight breeches, royal crown, and other regalia, but he took it in stride. It was a far cry from his call boy days in the shops at North Platte.

World War II was now a reality and, as Jeffers feared, we became a participant. We found ourselves faced with shortages—especially certain critical materials like rubber. A crisis was upon us which called for swift action. In September, 1942, Jeffers was selected by President Roosevelt to administer the vital synthetic rubber program. In characteristic fashion he tackled the job to the tune of "Let's get it done." Within a year the program was in high gear and "Jeff" was back with his beloved railroad. The rubber shortage had been "licked" and the war needs were being met with an even better product than before.

William Jeffers was a civic minded citizen who affiliated with various business and social clubs. But his hobby was the same as his job—railroading. He received recognition by various educational institutions for his contributions to American life. The degree of Doctor of Laws was conferred on him by Franklin and Marshall College, Creighton University, University of Wyoming, College of Idaho, and Notre Dame University. Like his predecessor, Carl Gray, he was denied much formal schooling but he advanced the cause of education in many ways, especially that type dealing with agriculture and the mechanical arts. He helped initiate a plan for granting Union Pacific scholarships for students planning to attend state agricultural colleges. These are granted each year to high school honor graduates in the eleven states in which the railroad operates. Thousands of young people have availed themselves of these awards.

Bill Jeffers retired from the presidency on February 1, 1946, but retained his contacts through his vice chairmanship of the Board of Directors. He was loath to quit working. In 1945, he bought a home in North Hollywood, California, so he could be close at hand to direct an immense flow of military personnel and war equipment. Later he took up residence in Pasadena. He headed up the Red Cross drive in Los Angeles in 1947, served as a director of the Los Angeles Turf Club at Santa Anita, and was a member of California's Commission on Organized Crime. He lent his support to every worthy civic enterprise. One of his last services was to act as chairman of the Citizens Smog Committee of Los Angeles.

Jeffers passed away in Pasadena on March 6, 1953. His wife, Lena, had preceded him in 1946. A long and successful career was ended but his life will be ever an inspiration for young people who are optimistic and believe in hard work. Norris Brown, former Nebraskan, wrote from Seattle:

"The youth of the country needs to know the virtues of men like William M. Jeffers. His habit of doing his part in all the tasks assigned kept him active and strong for more than half a century. He never faltered in his choice between ease and effort. Effort was his daily choice . . . Who can say such an example is not worthy of consideration by the old and emulation by the young?"

JOHN R. JIRDON, JR.

Livestock Raiser

JULY 8, 1895

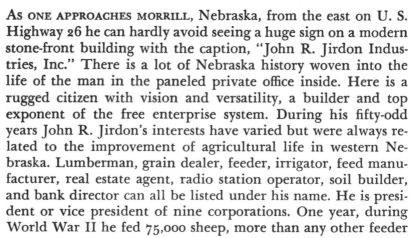

As one approaches Morrill, Nebraska, from the east on U. S. Highway 26 he can hardly avoid seeing a huge sign on a modern stone-front building with the caption, "John R. Jirdon Industries, Inc." There is a lot of Nebraska history woven into the life of the man in the paneled private office inside. Here is a rugged citizen with vision and versatility, a builder and top exponent of the free enterprise system. During his fifty-odd years John R. Jirdon's interests have varied but were always related to the improvement of agricultural life in western Nebraska. Lumberman, grain dealer, feeder, irrigator, feed manufacturer, real estate agent, radio station operator, soil builder, and bank director can all be listed under his name. He is president or vice president of nine corporations. One year, during World War II he fed 75,000 sheep, more than any other feeder in the United States at one time. "He and his family have 50 to 95 per cent interest in two thousand acres of irrigated land, and 16 thousand acres of wheat and grazing land, not to mention business holdings."

One of Jirdon's operations is the Kiowa Land and Livestock Company which he started, with a partner, a few years ago. Lambs are raised under "hot house" conditions for the early June market. With plenty of protective sheds there is a minimum of losses. One of these sheds is 140 by 204 feet, largest in the North Platte valley, and big enough for the feeding of 4,000 lambs. Some of his other interests are the Preston Wyoming Farms, Inc., the Pathfinder Land and Livestock Company, the Panhandle Land and Livestock Company, and the John R. Jirdon Livestock Company. Jirdon realizes full well, that livestock feeding is a hazardous business. The fluctuations in the grain and livestock markets are enough to "scare the pants" off the faint-hearted. But John Jirdon is not one to shed tears over losses though, naturally, he prefers black ink to red. He has been in the business long enough to expect an occasional slump in the market. But Jirdon plays his cards carefully and scientifically and the results prove his good management. Then, too, he doesn't put all his eggs in one basket. As to feeding operations he believes in two essentials, keeping his farms fertile, and utilizing the grain and roughage produced on these farms. Water and sunshine, he says, is all that nature provides in the valley, man must supply the other components. And, Jirdon has done just that. He plants crops such as alfalfa, sweet clover and grasses and plows these under together with artificial fertilizer and manure from the sheep sheds.

Much of his land has been leveled for irrigation and he not only uses the expensive equipment necessary for this work on his own farms but on his neighbors' as well. It is a big job but experience shows that it pays dividends. Like many successful operators, Jirdon deprecates the Government interfering with private business. He feels that individuals and communities ought to stand on their own feet as much as possible. A Republican in politics, he has opposed the steady growth of "Big Government" and what he considers its program of dictation. High income taxes have made expansion of corporations more difficult. "If you lose," he says, "Uncle Sam isn't your partner, but if you win, he wants the biggest share. It takes more than two good winnings to cancel out one loss."

John R. Jirdon, Jr. was born on a farm in Johnson County, Nebraska, and has lived in the state all his life. When young John was only four years old the family pulled stakes and headed west. John Jirdon, Sr. filed a tree claim 17 miles south of North Platte but a couple of dry years ended that venture. The Jirdons then moved to town and the father fed cattle for the divorced wife of William F. (Buffalo Bill) Cody. They lived in the cabin that the Codys had occupied when they were married. When spring came in 1901, John, Sr. decided on making the long jump to Oregon. With two covered wagons and two teams of horses the family set out following the general course of the North Platte River. Three weeks later, with money running short, they arrived at Bridgeport. Here the father and his oldest son, Walter, found work with their teams cleaning out an irrigation canal at $4 a day. After working a week lightning killed one of their horses and, since it took about $125 to replace it, a longer stay became necessary. In a few weeks the trip was resumed and on July 3 camp was made near Scottsbluff, which at that time had only a depot and a couple of wooden buildings on main street.

The Jirdons were told that Gering, across the river, was quite a bustling town and that a big Fourth of July celebration was scheduled there. This was something they could hardly pass up, for in those days it was the top event of the year. Here ended the Oregon movement for the Jirdons. In Gering the elder Jirdon met a Frank Sands who was building a canal and was offering high wages. He decided that Oregon could wait, and perhaps he was not too eager to take his ever-growing family so far on a "shoestring." Once again the father-son combination went to work and when cold weather came they hauled firewood to town for $2 a load. The family lived in a rented log cabin and grew to like the country better each day. During the summer, while living in Gering, young John and his brother Jerry herded milk cows outside of town for most of the residents. They were paid one dollar a head and this was a big help to the family budget. They also found time to explore the bluffs and swim in the canal.

For several years the elder Jirdon built canals, railroad grades, and for a time operated a sawmill, cutting logs for building bridges. During this period the family lived in camps but in 1907 moved into a sod house a mile north of Morrill. That year the father had bad luck on a canal contract job due to weather conditions and went broke. He then took a job as foreman on a canal project for the Government. Later, in 1910, he filed on a homestead six miles northwest of Morrill, one of the few left in the area.

While attending high school in Morrill, young John was school janitor at $15 a month. He also swept floors at the Methodist Church and ushered at the Opera House. After finishing the three-year course in 1912 he took a lumber yard job in Minatare at $40 a month. Here he put in long hours, unloading and loading lumber and coal during the day and taking care of the books at night. The next year he was sent to Angus, Nebraska, to manage a yard but returned to Minatare the following year to manage the yard there because of the illness of the manager. His introduction to the feed business was through W. R. Preston of Morrill with whom he spent much time on week-ends. Preston had taken on lumber, too, mostly as a retaliatory measure because a local lumber dealer was dabbling in grain. When only 20 years of age, Jirdon went into partnership with Preston, took time out to serve in World War I, and in 1924 bought out Preston's half of the business. Just prior to this the company went out of the lumber business, selling its stock in Morrill and also that in Scottsbluff where it had a yard for awhile.

Jirdon bought his first quarter-section in 1926, thirteeen miles southeast of Morrill, and went into partnership with a farmer to feed lambs on a 50-50 basis. Their first batch numbered 600. Today they are still working together and their feeding operation is a quarter-million dollar corporation. In the grain category Jirdon has elevators in five towns, two feed mills, one in Morrill and one in Gering, the Blue Jay Feeds, Inc., managed by Harold Roth. The Preston Wyoming Farms, Inc., on the edge of Torrington, Wyoming, in which he holds a half-interest, was originally a 540-acre tract. The growth of the town presented an opportunity to go into the townsite business. One block was donated for a county hospital. The Panhandle company operates 16,000 acres originally purchased from the Union Pacific Railroad. Ten thousand acres of this land are planted in wheat. The business of John R. Jirdon is conducted without salesmen on the road. Ninety per cent of the business is done by telephone and wire which, Mr. Jirdon believes, gives better prices to consumers. Personal contacts are made by sales managers and their assistants from time to time, but these are not selling trips.

Though Jirdon puts his hobby of soil building ahead of civic activities he has, by no means, ignored these. He has served on both the school and town boards and is a past president of the Associated Chambers of Commerce of the North Platte Valley. He has, likewise, been president of the Colorado-Nebraska Lamb Feeders Association, is a director of the Live Stock National Bank of Omaha and vice president of the First National Bank at Morrill. An active Republican, he has been a member of that party's State Central Committee. In 1920 he married a high school classmate, Gladys Marguerite Remender, and they have two married daughters. Hence, between his business, civic and family affairs Jirdon leads a busy life.

John R. Jirdon believes in being fair with his employees. His company boasts of having insurance and retirement plans "more generous than General Motors." During the depression years Jirdon kept his help on the payroll and was one of the last to make pay cuts. He recognizes that the profits under the free enterprise system are due, in large part, to faithful workers and the way to maintain loyalty is to treat them right. This hustler from western Nebraska, during his long versatile career, has proved his philosophy over and over again. Sound judgment, careful organization, hard work, fair play, and faith in the future have their rewards. Maintaining healthy industries in a community not only helps the man in business but brings prosperity, happiness and pride to all citizens. Some have called his success "Jirdon luck" but those who know him best call it good management.

SAMUEL ROY McKELVIE

Farm Publisher

APRIL 15, 1881

SAM McKELVIE has had three loves: publishing, politics, and ranching. The latter he enjoys most. His politics included membership in the Lincoln city council, a term in the legislature, the office of lieutenant governor, and two terms as governor. He has held no aspirations for office on the national level. In fact, he turned down an offer to be President Hoover's Secretary of Agriculture. This is unusual, for most men when once immersed in the political pot are eager to keep on boiling. Perhaps the dreary state of agriculture in 1929 was a deterrent to Sam, but more than likely he wanted to get on with his plans for raising cattle. Anyway, that is what he did after serving a short while, though reluctantly, on the President's Federal Farm Board. Politics and publishing had taken a big chunk out of his life. He would wait no longer to do that which he liked best.

McKelvie is a man of principle in whom his associates have

always had great confidence. He was never carried away by emotional demagogues preaching doctrines of hate nor by reformers with panaceas for "saving the country." When a wave of hysteria swept the nation following World War I, culminating in a revival of the Ku Klux Klan and other movements by self-styled patriots, he vigorously opposed such actions. Sam McKelvie believes in the fundamental freedoms, especially religious liberty. Freedom, in his opinion, is not the monopoly of the majority but minorities are equally entitled to constitutional safeguards. He speaks out boldly in defense of these rights—and Sam is a top-notch speaker.

Samuel Roy, son of Samuel and Jennie Glandon McKelvie, was born on a farm near Fairfield, Nebraska, April 15, 1881. That name was soon reduced to just plain "Sam" and to most people he has been that ever since. Today he signs it that way. His father was a breeder of purebred Poland China hogs and for more than a half-century was a regular exhibitor. In later years he and young Sam received the annual award of the Block and Bridle Club at the University of Nebraska. This award was given to those considered to have contributed most to the livestock industry of the state. The elder McKelvie, also, raised Red Poll cattle successfully. Hence, Sam was initiated into the livestock business at an early age. When only 13 his father sent him out to buy feeder cattle and he did so well the practice was continued. Many boys who grow up on the land hanker to get away from it. Sam loved the country life and all through his public career yearned to return to the rural atmosphere.

Young McKelvie got his first learning in a rural school after which he went through the local high school. He was not too concerned about higher education but did attend the University of Nebraska and the Lincoln Business College. A degree did not seem important to him, and in his case it probably made little difference. He was eager to set to work and his training, both practical and formal, was sufficient to do what he had in mind. Max Coffey, writing in the *Omaha World-Herald,* says that "Sam McKelvie is one of those few peculiarly-gifted individuals who have been able to direct their energies to getting out of life just about what they want." Proof that he succeeded is evident by the fact that he was one of five granted an honorary doctor's degree by the University of Nebraska in 1951. His, of course, was in agriculture.

In 1902, at the age of 21, Sam set out to make his "fortune."

He took a job as a livestock field man (advertising solicitor) for the *Twentieth Century Farmer*, a supplement of the *Omaha Bee*. One day his father dropped a remark about Nebraska lacking a good farm paper. There was a weekly called the *Nebraska Farmer*, founded in 1859 by Robert Furnas at Brownville, but it was later moved to Lincoln. According to the elder McKelvie it did not meet the needs of the farmers. Sam decided he wanted to own that paper and bring it into line with up-to-date agricultural education. In 1905 he left the *Bee* and became its editor. The year before he had married Martha De Arnold and they now settled down in Lincoln.

By 1907 McKelvie was ready to buy the *Nebraska Farmer* and he borrowed most of the $10,000 purchase price. He proceeded, forthwith, to make it the leading farm paper in the state. Its circulation rose steadily, 15,000 in 1908 to over 125,000 in 1938, and continues to this day under his management. Even through the depression years the farmers hung on to their *Nebraska Farmer*. Through this publication Sam made himself and his views familiar to the people of the state and surrounding territory. Its lively stories, pungent editorials, helpful hints, reports on farm prices, and even its advertisements furnished heaps of reading on cold winter evenings.

Sam now got other ideas. He had an ambition to become governor of his state but knew he must first serve an apprenticeship in other offices before trying for the "jackpot." He served a term, 1908–09, on the Lincoln city council and then was sent to the legislature. Two years later, 1912, he was chosen lieutenant governor. This office offered little to challenge the young Republican but as presiding officer of the senate he made acquaintances and gained valuable experience. In 1918, at the age of 37, Sam McKelvie was elected governor and was, at the time, the youngest chief state executive in the nation. He was re-elected in 1920 and thus he had four years to carry through his program.

And McKelvie had a program. His administration is generally considered a constructive one, in sharp contrast to the national scene at that time. He believed in the adage that there should be "more business in government and less government in business," and lived up to it. He believed that state administration, to be efficient, should be well organized and he directed his efforts to that end. The technical age was bringing many material changes and Nebraska, at the crossroads of the nation,

[117]

must keep pace with the times. Several important moves were made. First, a badly needed new state capitol was authorized, to cost $10,000,000, under a pay-as-you-go plan. Finished in 1934, it is considered one of the finest buildings of its kind in the nation, if not in the whole world. And it was entirely paid for when completed.

The antiquated Constitution of 1875 was in dire need of overhauling. A constitutional convention was held, 1919–20, and drew up 41 amendments to bring that document up-to-date. All were approved by the electorate. An effort was made to include one calling for a unicameral legislature but without success. This proposal had to wait until a later date. There had been much talk about the need for reorganization of the administrative offices in the capitol but it took the McKelvie leadership to get action. New offices had been added in harum-scarum fashion presenting a sprawling situation. The 1919 Legislature enacted the Civil Administrative Code, combining twenty-two state commissions and bureaus into six departments with the heads of each to be appointed by and responsible to the governor. The state laws were also recodified and made more intelligible. The need for better recreational facilities was recognized by the initiation of a system of state parks, the results of which are becoming more apparent each day.

The coming of the motor vehicle and the new emphasis on education made a new road system imperative. The people had to have "better roads for better schools" and better means to "go to town." A comprehensive system of highway improvement was inaugurated, also on a pay-as-you-go basis. The gasoline tax had arrived to help finance this work. Pressure was on, too, for a soldiers' bonus but under the state constitution bonds could not be issued for that purpose. However, a fund of $2,-000,000 was created through direct taxes, the income from which has been used for the relief of needy veterans and their dependents. Sam McKelvie had reason to be proud of his four years' stewardship as governor.

He was ready now to withdraw from the political arena and take up his third love—ranching. He continued with his publishing but kept an eye open for a desirable "spread," as the cattlemen call it. Returning from a week's hunting in the sand-hills country in 1931 Sam and his wife spotted the place, near Valentine, where they wanted to make their home. In characteristic fashion he quickly bought the ranch and set to work replacing the old ranch house and homesteaders' shacks with attractive and practical buildings. Mrs. McKelvie named it "BY THE WAY RANCH" and also supplied the idea for their brand, "VIA." She had not been too eager to leave Lincoln and take up ranch life but soon developed a liking for it as keen as that of her husband. On these 10,000 acres of grazing and hay land McKelvie ran a herd of 500 registered cattle, the pride of the sandhills and far beyond.

Sam, with his knowledge of agriculture, recognized the sandhills to be a rich package of resources for cattlemen. Max Coffey writes:

"These included the 'sea of grass' that blanketed the hills; the lush wet meadows that yielded nutritious hay crops for carrying stock over winter; the abundance of water in cool, clear streams and thousands of glistening lakes. In fact, the whole sandhills area may truthfully be said to be floating on an ocean on underground water. This is, in McKelvie's label, 'God's Own Cow Country.' "

When Sam McKelvie moved into the sandhills he found the cattle market in a bad way. This was expected as the country was in the grip of a great depression. What distressed him more was the lack of consideration given sandhills' cattle in the feeder markets. He set to work to do something about it. Early in 1938 a ranchers' meeting was held in Valentine which resulted in the formation of the Sand Hills Feeder Cattle Producers Association, later changed to the shorter title, Sand Hills Cattle Association. Sam was the sparkplug in this move and held the office of president for ten years. This Association has had a remarkable record since its inception. In its bulletin is listed the name of each member along with the cattle he has for sale, breed, number, sex, age, brand and location of the ranch. Today the bulletin is issued twice each month to some 20,000 feeders all over the country. Its 750 members market in the course of a year over 100,000 feeder cattle. The upgrading of sandhills cattle has gone on steadily and the improvement in quality has netted the ranchers "good money." The Association has knit the cattlemen closer together in their common enterprise as well as in a social way. It is not surprising that McKelvie wrote in the summer of 1950 that "of all my activities raising and showing purebred Herefords is the one I enjoy most."

Sam's worth in the cattle industry is further attested by his election, in 1937, to the presidency of the American Hereford

Association, the largest organization of cattle breeders in the world. He, also, has had two six-year terms on the Board of Directors. It goes without saying that he has always been active in social, fraternal, educational and religious affairs. His memberships include: Chamber of Commerce, University Club, Masons, Elks, Odd Fellows and the Methodist Church.

Only recently McKelvie, regretfully, sold his ranch to two of his neighbors but reserved the use of his spacious home. His fine cattle were sold at auction in one of the greatest pure-bred sales ever held in the state. The burdens of management had become too great for his years. He had offered to give the ranch to the University but complications developed over the conditions of transfer, so to avoid harmful publicity, he withdrew the offer. This native son has truly had a distinguished and useful career. He has brought honor to the state and to himself—a representative Nebraskan of the first order.

BUTLER BUCHANAN MILTONBERGER

National Guardsman

AUGUST 31, 1897

THE NEBRASKA NATIONAL GUARD has played many important
roles in the history of the state. This military unit has been a
trouble-shooting organization when domestic troubles have
arisen, and the first to respond in time of war. It rendered
valiant service in the Civil War, the Indian wars on the plains,
and the Philippines during the Spanish-American War and the
Philippine Insurrection. When trouble broke out on the Mexican border the Guard went into action. Shortly thereafter it
was fighting in France. During World War II it bore more than
its share of heavy fighting on the battlefields of Europe. This
citizen army deserves more credit than is usually accorded it.

Many Nebraskans can look back proudly on their records
with the Guard. One of these is Butler Miltonberger of North
Platte. He saw his first military service as a private with the unit

in June, 1916, on the Mexican border following the raids of the bandit Pancho Villa. The next year he was overseas with the 4th Division in World War I and went through the Argonne campaign where he advanced to first sergeant. Remaining in the Guard after the war he was commissioned a first lieutenant in the Infantry of the Nebraska unit on May 12, 1923, and was made a captain later that year. Further promotions came from time to time: major on January 14, 1933, lieutenant colonel, October 7, 1940, and shortly before the attack on Pearl Harbor he was raised to temporary colonel. On March 17, 1945, Miltonberger was made a temporary brigadier general and a temporary major general, February 1, 1946. These advancements came as a result of faithful and effective service both in time of peace and war. Like many non-professional soldiers he proved that civilians, who are willing to give of their time for training, can be ready for duty in time of crisis.

Butler Miltonberger commanded Company "D," 134th Infantry Regiment for ten years. He was highly commended for his part in such emergencies as the riots in Omaha and the Republican River flood, both in 1935. His performance in connection with Army maneuvers at Fort Riley, Kansas, in 1937 and at Camp Ripley, Minnesota, in 1940 brought further praise. The 134th was mobilized in December, 1940, while he was attending Battalion Commanders' Staff School at Fort Benning, Georgia. In February, 1941, he took command of the 1st Battalion and the Selectee Training Regiment of the 134th and in May the entire regiment. Training was carried on at several centers: Fort Ord and Camp Luis Obispo, California, Camp Rucker, Alabama, Camp Butner, North Carolina, and in May, 1944, the Regiment was sent overseas, arriving in France July 5.

No time was lost in sending the Regiment into action. Three days after arrival in France orders were received by the 134th to relieve other troops. From then on until the Elbe River was reached in May, 1945, the Regiment was actively engaged in operations against the enemy except for occasional rest periods. Each battalion was alternated, hence two battalions were constantly on the line. The operations of the 134th have been written up in *All Hell Can't Stop Us,* by Miltonberger and Major Huston, the latter now a professor of history at Purdue University. It is a thrilling story, giving the details of each engagement. The Nebraskans are especially associated with action at St. Lo, Vire, Mortain, Montargis, Morhange, Sarreguemines,

Bastogne, Alsace, Venlo, and from Geilenkirchen to the Elbe River. In the spring of 1945 Miltonberger was made Assistant Division Commander of the 35th Infantry Division, of which the 134th Regiment was a part, in recognition of his superb qualities as a fearless leader.

Born in North Platte, Nebraska, on August 31, 1897, Butler Buchanan Miltonberger grew up in that section of the state famous as the home of "Buffalo Bill." Undoubtedly his imagination was stirred by the exploits of this dashing plainsman as well as stories of the Indian wars. As a young chap he heard the sagas of the Spanish-American War and the Philippine Insurrection. It is not unusual that he interested himself in things of a military character and at the age of 18 joined the Guard. From that moment he has divided his time between civil and military affairs. He has had many unusual experiences but the gruelling campaign from Normandy to the Elbe tops them all. Here he proved his leadership and demonstrated, the hard way, the value of efficient training. Lawrence Youngman of the *Omaha World-Herald* staff, assigned to cover the movements of the Regiment, wrote: "It has set for Nebraska a new standard of courage and gallantry and determination and military efficiency and leadership." In the initial baptism of fire before St. Lo the Guardsmen proved conclusively that they could slug it out with the enemy as ably as regular troops.

Miltonberger was a stickler for careful and coordinated planning and highly respected as a disciplinarian. Just before the push on St. Lo he called his technical sergeants together and explained to them the assignment and stressed the importance of each unit carrying out its own responsibility. The results show how well they had learned their lessons. The enemy was using hedgerow to hedgerow defense and the Nebraska "troops were constantly subjected to heavy mortar, artillery and small arms fire." Despite this tough resistance and heavy casualties they made steady progress and their patrols were the first to enter the city. After the capture of St. Lo the Regiment was assigned the nasty job of holding it. From July 19 to July 28 it was the target of heavy German artillery and mortar fire but the 134th held fast. The place "lost all semblance of a city" and "aside from soldiers, there was not even a stray cat in the place."

It is beyond the scope of this account to follow the operations of the 134th in Europe but it should be emphasized that this Regiment was in the thick of the conflict. Youngman wrote:

"Day and night the fighting went on. But the former Nebraska National Guard regiment was indomitable. Under the leadership of officers and non-coms who were predominantly Nebraskans, it had but one thought: to go forward." And go forward it did. After St. Lo the going continued to be rugged, but once the German retreat was in full swing the Regiment soon found itself in Eastern France. One experience stands out among many others. On September 15 the Mayor of Nancy presented Colonel Miltonberger, at the city hall, a parchment scroll expressing appreciation to the liberators of the city. The Mayor said that the swift advance of the 134th had saved Nancy from the wrecking crew of the Nazis. To the end of the War in Europe the Nebraskans proved their gallantry and made their home state proud of them.

The Regiment was returned to Camp Breckenridge after the War and in November, 1945, Miltonberger was assigned to the Secretary of War's Separation Board in Washington. Shortly thereafter he was named by President Truman to be Chief of the National Guard Bureau and was advanced to temporary Major General. He did a "bang-up" job in this office. "The War Department had assigned the National Guard the mission of an M-Day Force, trained, equipped and immediately available for service with the Regular Army in the event of aggression by an enemy nation. This M-Day Force was given a quota of 682,000 men, almost three times the authorized strength of the pre-war Guard."

Miltonberger set to work vigorously. He instituted a national information and advertising campaign to rebuild the prestige of the National Guard and explain its increased importance to our security in a hostile world. The best in the way of equipment was furnished the Guard units and a "supply, procurement and maintenance system paralleling that of the regular Army was put into effect." Plans for summer field training, first since 1940, were drawn up under his direction. Through a series of conferences, Miltonberger brought "a closer relationship between the National Guard Bureau and the several states as well as encouraging cooperation and respect among the components of the Army." In short, he streamlined the Guard, dressed it up, and made it a more effective part of our national defense set-up.

He was forced to retire, September 30, 1947, because of a lung condition but by that time "more than 100,000 men were receiving regular instruction and training." After spending some time in Walter Reed Hospital Miltonberger settled down again in North Platte with the permanent rating of Major General, retired. But, in private life he is never idle. A member of the State Engineering Staff, he divides his time between Lincoln and North Platte. Also, he is active in the affairs of his community and is both a Mason and an Elk. Twice married, he has a daughter, Helen Irene, by his first marriage.

Miltonberger has won many decorations: for service on the Mexican Border, in World War I and World War II, and in reorganizing the National Guard. These include Legion of Merit with 2 clusters, Silver Star, Bronze Star Medal with 3 clusters, and the Distinguished Service Medal. Foreign decorations include French Legion of Honor, French Croix de Guerre with Palm, Netherlands Order of Orange—Nassau, and the Luxembourg Croix de Guerre. There are many others.

Our Country could well afford more leaders like Major General Miltonberger who are willing to take time from their regular work to train and direct training for the defense of the Nation. His example should inspire all of us to be better citizens and assume a more positive role for the maintenance of our democratic system. The blood bath endured by the 134th Infantry Regiment and the heroic fight it made against the Nazi hordes wrote a new and glorious chapter in Nebraska history. We ought to be proud of their achievements and the man who so ably led them.

JULIUS STERLING MORTON

Agriculturist

APRIL 22, 1832 · APRIL 27, 1902

MANY SPECIAL DAYS are to be found on the calendar but few are more meaningful than Arbor Day. In Nebraska this means April 22, the birthday of J. Sterling Morton, the founder of that day. This is the day when old and young take time out to plant trees and this activity has done much for a state that, originally, was largely treeless. Morton's beautiful home at Nebraska City, Arbor Lodge, was given to the state and is now a state park where thousands make pilgrimages annually. His bronze statue is one of two Nebraska Greats that now stand in Statuary Hall in the rotunda of the National Capitol. This former cabinet member, agriculturist, publisher, and active Democrat led a busy life in his adopted state and attained a national reputation. The recognition extended him was richly deserved.

Julius Sterling Morton was born in Adams, New York, April 22, 1832. His grandfather Abner Morton, a lawyer, had moved to Detroit, Michigan, where he became the first editor of the *Free Press*. His parents moved there when Sterling was quite small and his father, Julius Dewey Morton, prospered in the new state. Young Morton attended the University of Michigan and Union College, being graduated from the latter school in 1854. Shortly thereafter he married Caroline Joy of a prominent Detroit family and, on their wedding day, set out for the new territory of Nebraska.

This honeymoon trip was not entirely a pleasant one but it did have its thrills. The first winter in Nebraska was spent at Bellevue where the young couple arrived on November 10, 1854, according to the first issue of the *Bellevue Palladium*. After a rather hectic winter spent in a log cabin they moved down to Kearny, later to be incorporated as Nebraska City. Morton began at once to write editorials for the *Nebraska City News* for which he received $60 a month. In this way his ideas were pumped into the new environment and his influence felt. This young college man got his feet on the ground early. He had business sense and he had common sense. He recognized the importance of the common virtues. From the start Morton envisaged the worth of the country and its possibilities from an agricultural point of view, especially if sound conservation principles were practiced. He set the pattern and the impact of his ideas became more widespread as time passed.

A few days after the arrival in Nebraska City, Mrs. Morton returned to Michigan accompanied on the steamboat by her husband as far as St. Louis. After the birth of their first child, Joy Morton, she and her father and infant son traveled to Nebraska covering the last 90 miles to Nebraska City by wagon. During his wife's absence Morton purchased a sizable tract of land including the 65 acres of what is now Arbor Lodge and constructed a frame house. During this time he lived, "bachelor style," in a small log house on his land and continued to write for the paper while supervising operations on the farm. He was very proud of his house and years later reminisced: "From the site of old Fort Kearny, now Nebraska City, the rich emerald sod of the prairies stretched away to the base of the Rocky mountains, uncleft by a plowshare and unvexed by the munching teeth of the lowing herds. There was no frame house between the one in which this is written and the Rocky mountains,—not one."

Changes in the house were made, piece-meal fashion, from

time to time as the family grew in size and the wealth of Morton increased. As his prestige grew he had many visitors to entertain and the Lodge was adapted to meet the needs. Following his death in 1902 the home was remodeled with additional building by his son, Joy Morton. At the time of the transfer of the property to the state it was a 52-room mansion. Even during Morton's lifetime the home is said to have been "the greatest private show spot in Nebraska—in the middle west."

Though involved in politics throughout his life, Morton's greatest contribution to the state was in the field of scientific agriculture. He planted a "veritable garden in the midst of the prairie country." He brought in various kinds of trees from other areas and demonstrated that Nebraska's face could be changed. Success crowned his efforts in growing fruit trees and he set the pace in making southeast Nebraska a great orchard region. Morton was active in several agricultural societies furnishing the leadership necessary to stimulate the use of new methods. Exhibits of Nebraska products were displayed at fairs and festivals, both within and outside the Territory, and even abroad. Morton was an original member of the Territorial Horticultural Society and of the Nebraska Territorial Board of Agriculture. He served as president of each. After Nebraska became a state in 1867 his activities continued with even greater zeal, and he was a prime mover in developing the State Fair. In fact, no important meeting relating to agriculture was quite in order without his presence.

Morton did not meet with overwhelming success in politics. He was a conservative Democrat and most of his life the Republicans "ran the show" on the national level. Only during his first years in Nebraska and the two separated Cleveland administrations did Democrats have a chance. He served in the territorial legislatures of 1855 and 1857 and was appointed secretary of the territory by President Buchanan. Twice he served as acting territorial governor. Four times the state gubernatorial nominee and twice a candidate for Congress, Morton failed, by narrow margins, to be elected. His name was ever in evidence when the legislature balloted for United States senators though he was never selected. But, he was in there "pitching" all the time. Through his newspaper, the *Nebraska City News*, he voiced his opinions on the issues of the day. A "hard money" and sound banking advocate, he was opposed by the inflationary wing of his own party. He bitterly fought Bryan on the "free silver" question even to the point of publishing a special paper, *The Con-servative,* for that purpose.

Perhaps the highlight of Morton's public career came in 1893 when President Cleveland appointed him Secretary of Agriculture, the first Nebraskan selected for a cabinet post. Here he had an opportunity to serve the people he knew the best. His ideas on what was best for agriculture were well fixed in the mind of this rugged 60-year-old pioneer. His grandson, Sterling Morton III, sums up his philosophy as follows: "He realized that agriculture was the very foundation of our national life, that the farmer should have every proper encouragement, every proper opportunity to become a better, more prosperous farmer. But he had little patience with those who exploited the real needs of the farmer, who sought to destroy the traditional independence of the rural population." He had gone to Washington at a critical time when panic and uncertainty gripped the country. It was only natural that this believer in practical economy should follow a prudent course. During his four-year term the appropriations for his department were $11,179,000, and of this sum he returned to the Treasury about a fifth of the appropriations. Even so he accomplished much and introduced several new practices. One of these was the issuing of the *Farmers' Bulletins* to give this group new ideas on various phases of farming to increase their production. He opposed the free distribution of seeds and plants calling it an extravagance that should be "utterly abolished." Morton reported: "It is safe to say that 1,800,-000 citizens received seeds, but only 940 persons acknowledged their receipt—generally with a request for more seeds."

Records of the State Board of Agriculture show that it was Morton who submitted a resolution suggesting that April 10, 1872, be set aside as Arbor Day. A prize of $100 was to be offered to the county agricultural society planting the largest number of trees on that day, and a farm library worth $25 to the person planting the largest number. Governor Furnas issued a proclamation to that effect and the legislature enacted a law making Arbor Day a legal holiday. Morton's birthday, April 22, was selected later for this observance in Nebraska. Several other states followed Nebraska's example for an Arbor Day. In 1884 Morton launched a movement to make it a nation-wide observance. While Secretary of Agriculture he pushed it still farther. The schools quickly responded to the idea. As the years passed the benefits became more and more obvious. Had the people been more conservation-minded the results would have been even more gratifying. In Morton's day exploitation was our national habit. The Roosevelt programs were really a follow-up on his conservation and rehabilitation plans.

At the close of his term as Secretary of Agriculture, J. Sterling Morton retired to his beloved Arbor Lodge. From this point he continued to express his views on the political, economic, and social questions of the day until his death, April 27, 1902. He was a great collector of documents and his collection filled eleven huge boxes including "correspondence with people famous in government, literary and scientific circles." The Morton records constitute a treasure chest of Nebraska history. These papers furnished much of the information for Dr. James C. Olson, now Superintendent of the State Historical Society, when he wrote an excellent biography of this great Nebraskan a few years ago. Morton, himself, projected an extended history of Nebraska in 1897 but died after completing the first volume. Two more volumes were published under the editorship of Albert Watkins. Morton's wife Caroline died in 1881, leaving four sons, Joy, Paul, Mark, and Carl. She had been a splendid wife and mother. The children grew in stature and through their public and private endeavors brought additional recognition to the Morton name.

J. Sterling Morton's principles, like the trees that perpetuate his memory, were deep-rooted. Again to quote his grandson, Sterling Morton, III: "His ideas, his very ways of life were conservative. . . . His conservatism held fast to that which the past had proven good, yet he was anxious to embrace principles which the future might prove to be good." These words, penned by Morton himself, appear on a bronze statue erected at Arbor Lodge by the Arbor Day Memorial Association:

> "Love of Home is Primary Patriotism.
> Other Holidays Repose upon the Past;
> Arbor Day Proposes for the Future."

JOHN GNEISENAU NEIHARDT

Poet Laureate

JANUARY 8, 1881

ON THE CAMPUS OF Nebraska State Teachers College at Wayne stands a three-story, U-shaped women's dormitory called Neihardt Hall. It is doubtful if the co-eds living here from year to year know much about the man for whom it is named. Someone has probably told them that a poet of some renown by the name of John G. Neihardt attended school here when it was a private institution called Nebraska Normal College. They may have learned that he is Nebraska's Poet Laureate, a title conferred upon him in 1921 by the legislature. This was the first time such an honor had been granted by any governing body in the history of America.

Many high school and college students have studied his epic poems as class assignments but probably not to the extent that they got the "feel" that Neihardt intended. Perhaps a few have captured the full meaning of his literature. If so, they should have more understanding of and more sympathy for our first Americans, the Indians. Nebraskans are proud that this "bubbling little man . . . with a sweep of thick gray hair and penetrating gray eyes under craggy brows" spent many years in their midst. This tireless worker has "sparked both life and literature with his intense enthusiasm" and helped put Nebraska on the map. Old Timers like to tell how young Neihardt paid his tuition by ringing the big class bell twice every 50 minutes beginning at 6:30 each morning. They say, too, that he was a good story-teller and sometimes wrote saucy verses. That would make him somewhat akin to James Whitcomb Riley the Hoosier poet. Though he possesses a keen sense of humor and has his moments of levity, you soon discover he has a message to deliver. You have the feeling that he is serving you a concentrate, the result of long and intensive labor. And that is exactly what he is doing and his eyes sparkle and snap when he speaks.

Neihardt once said: "As a poet, one is increasingly aware of the wonder of things. It's like you had a tonic that's done you good and you want to tell others about it. You want to share this happiness." The ambition of the poet is "to continue to become a little more understanding." And this understanding, according to his philosophy, can be attained only by close association with one's subject. It was on-the-spot research that enabled him to write from the depth of experience. Only by living among the Indians could he have produced his masterpiece, *A Cycle of the West*. But, Neihardt loves life, and though his years have been devoted to literary pursuits, he has found time for many other activities. His most recent avocation is the raising of beef cattle. His wife, Mona, is a sculptress of some renown and they have reared and educated four children—Enid, Sigurd, Hilda and Alice.

John Gneisenau Neihardt was born in an unplastered one-room house on a rented farm near Sharpsburg, Illinois, January 8, 1881. The family moved shortly to Springfield and lived there until the fall of 1886, then migrated to Rooks County, Kansas. A year was spent here with John's maternal grandparents in a sod house. The next five years, 1887–1892, they made their home in Kansas City, Missouri, then came the trek to the little town of Wayne, Nebraska. It was here that young Neihardt began his literary endeavors writing his first verses at the age of 12. He enrolled at the Normal College, finished the teachers' course in

1896, and the scientific curriculum a year later. He made a specialty of Latin, spending as much as five hours a day on that subject. Neihardt also began a systematic and intensive reading of the classics, and even studied Greek so that he might familiarize himself with the original masterpieces of that literature.

The school year, 1897–1898, found him teaching a country school but the open road beckoned the young scholar. The following summer he tramped through Kansas and Missouri getting "experience." By the time Neihardt was 20 he had tried his hand at many things, farm hand, hod carrier, clerk, office boy, marble polisher, and stenographer. He even spent two months as City Hall reporter on the *Omaha Daily News.* His parents moved to Bancroft, Nebraska, in 1901. This town was at the edge of the Omaha Indian reservation and here he found his golden (or *copper*) opportunity. During the next six years Neihardt lived more or less among the Indians. He assisted in the office of an Indian trader in Bancroft handling Indian leases, collecting, and doing various odd jobs. He even "took a whirl" at journalism, organizing a stock company which purchased the *Bancroft Blade,* a weekly paper. Neihardt was with this publication only one year. He apparently was bored with the job except for writing editorials at which he was very good. His chief interest seems to have been making intimate acquaintance with Indian life.

Actually, while living at Bancroft, Neihardt was laying plans for his masterpiece. "Wishing to write an epic concerning the westward advance in America to the Pacific, and to familiarize himself with the territory which would form the background of the epic, Neihardt traveled through the country and descended the Missouri River from the headwaters at Fort Benton, Montana, in an open boat. Thorough research brought forth exploits of the trappers and traders who explored the wilderness from the British boundary to Mexico and from the Missouri River to the Pacific Ocean." Neihardt says that "Literature in itself is nothing. It's life that counts." The many hours he spent around camp fires getting acquainted with the Indians, their history and habits, and the hundreds of miles traveled tracing the trails of the pioneers, furnished the young poet with sources for writing unobtainable elsewhere. But, best of all, it gave him perspective, a 3-dimensional picture of the stories he planned to write.

As a boy Neihardt had dabbled in poetry. Later he turned to short stories and a number of these appeared in the "leading slick magazines." However, he had a feeling that he must concentrate on poetry to do his best work. He began work on his epic poems in 1912. The "songs" that make up the *Cycle* appeared as follows: *The Song of Hugh Glass,* 1915; *The Song of Three Friends,* 1919 (awarded $500 prize as best volume of verse by the Poetry Society of America); *The Song of the Indian Wars,* 1925; *The Song of the Messiah,* 1935; and *The Song of Jed Smith,* 1941. This group of long narrative poems was published in 1949 as *A Cycle of the West* and established Neihardt as one of the outstanding literary men of our time. He has written many other works of poetry and prose. A novel of the Sioux, *When the Tree Flowered,* is his latest book, appearing in 1951. Another of his prose productions, *Black Elk Speaks,* is based on the story given him at Pine Ridge Reservation in South Dakota by a "real Indian holy man," a cousin of Chief Crazy Horse. He took two of his daughters with him on this mission and they lived in tepees while gathering data, much to the delight of the Indians. Neihardt says this was "the most remarkable experience" of his life.

The United States Bureau of Indian Affairs thinks highly of Neihardt. And well it should for he has been of great assistance to this agency. He was Director of Information, 1944–1946, and Field Representative, 1946–1948, for the Office of Indian Affairs in Chicago. He understands the problems confronting the Indians and they trust him. They know, that among the Whites, they never had a more loyal friend.

Neihardt has had a varied writing career. He has written literary criticisms for the *New York Times* and the *Minneapolis Journal,* and from 1926 to 1938 was literary editor of the *St. Louis Post-Dispatch.* Recognition in the way of honorary degrees has been conferred by the University of Nebraska, University of Missouri and Creighton University of Omaha. He is an interesting speaker and has made appearances on many university and college platforms. Since 1948 Neihardt has been poet-in-residence and lecturer in English at the University of Missouri. The Neihardts for many years made their home at Branson, Missouri, in the Shepherd of the Hills country.

Only one who has been intimately associated with John G. Neihardt can do justice to an evaluation of this great literary figure. This noble soul has a quality of character difficult to define. He has ever been the dreamer, the idealist, the mystic, any yet he is extremely practical in many ways. A recent writer makes this comment: "Nowadays, as his schedule of work is more varied, John Neihardt may be found poring over magazines devoted to the problems of raising livestock; or he may be checking the meter and rhythm of a poem written by a pupil; he may be working on polishing up some gem stones; or he might be looking over some of the mechanical gadgets he invented in his youth before he had a dream that motivated him to become a poet."

Yes, John Gneisenau Neihardt has done a "heap o' livin'" and, in spite of his advancing years, is still going strong. This bushy-haired little man has gotten much out of life and he has made life worth living for a lot of other people. He loves nature, people, books, and most of all of course his family, which in spite of a busy life, has always been his Number One interest.

GEORGE WILLIAM NORRIS

Insurgent Republican

JULY 11, 1861 · SEPTEMBER 2, 1944

GEORGE W. NORRIS kept Nebraska on the front page of America for nearly a half-century. Seldom does a man of independent thought and action, so indifferent to the party machine, manage to stay in public office. This modest "Gentleman from Nebraska" was a fighter from the word "go" and his constituents loved it, even though the causes for which he fought did not always bring special benefits to the state. Editor Charles S. Ryckman of the *Fremont* (Nebraska) *Tribune,* in his Pulitzer winning editorial in 1930 said: "His people take delight in setting him on the heels of the ruling powers, whether of government, of finance or of industry. The more he makes himself obnoxious to a political party, to a national administration or to Wall Street, the better they like him." How true a statement when, came war, prosperity, or depression, they continued to send him to Washington.

For forty years he served either in the House of Representatives or the Senate without a break.

Ryckman makes this summarization:

"Nebraska derives a great deal of pleasure out of shoving George W. Norris down the great American throat. He has been an effective emetic in republican and democratic administrations alike, has worried every president from Taft to Hoover. His retirement from the senate, whether voluntary or forced, would be welcomed in more quarters than that of any of his colleagues.

"The people of Nebraska know this, and enjoy it. Every time Norris baits the power trust or lambasts the social lobby, Nebraska gets the same amusement out of his antics that a small boy gets out of sicing a dog on an alley cat. When he shies a brickbat at a president, Nebraska has as much fun as a kid pushing over an outhouse.

"It has been said of Norris that he has cast more negative votes against winning causes and more affirmative votes for lost causes than any other man in the senate. But every time he succeeds in pestering his prey until it turns around and snarls back at him, the chuckles can be heard all the way from Council Bluffs to Scottsbluff."

Up to the New Deal days Norris had fought for many lost causes, but during the Thirties he was to witness changes that turned many of these into victories. He was now on the offensive team and the legislative mill ground out act after act incorporating the program for which he had fought so long. Agriculture and Labor both shared in the benefits and even Business, though loath to admit it, was given a "shot in the arm." Standards of living were raised for millions of people who had never known the real meaning of economic democracy.

It would be easy to say that the character of this man of integrity was the result of the grub-hoe labor spent on an Ohio farm while helping a widowed mother raise a large family. This unbroken stretch of hard work, undoubtedly, prompted many of his later stands, giving him sympathy for farm debtors and workers generally. But there seems to have been something inherent in Norris that would have made him champion of the underdog regardless of his own early experiences. And it should be said that persistency, not stubbornness, was his dominant trait. He was willing to compromise and take less to secure part of his program, but this liberal never lost sight of the big objective.

George William Norris was born July 11, 1861, near Clyde, Ohio, some sixty miles west of Cleveland. His father died when

George, youngest of a large family, was only three. The widow set about making a home for her children and since George's only brother John was killed in the war, Will, as he was called as a boy, became her mainstay. Though very poor, Mary Norris was determined that her children have the advantages of an education above the grammar grades. George attended the local school during the winter months and worked for neighboring farmers during the summers. He learned to be frugal, saved his money, for he decided quite early to be a lawyer. One of his teachers, I. D. Speidell, encouraged him in his purpose and helped him to become a member of the Carmel Debating Society. Here he got his first experience in parliamentary procedure and in matching his wits against other minds. He also became convinced that the Republican party had the best program.

In the fall of 1877, at the age of 16, he and two sisters enrolled at Baldwin University (now Baldwin-Wallace College) in Berea near Cleveland. Brother John had attended there earlier and that, together with the fact that this was the "poor boy's school," determined this move. The three Norrises rented the three-room upper floor of a house on the edge of town and proceeded to "keep house" in a cooperative effort to conserve their meager funds. In spite of the need for careful economy they "had fun" along with the serious matter of pursuing an education. George was a diligent student and his high grades attest the fact. He joined the literary society and took an active part. Though he spent only one year on this campus, he always had pleasant memories for the time spent there.

Needing to replenish his school "stake" Norris taught several terms and then enrolled at Northern Indiana Normal School (now Valparaiso University), known as the "Poor Man's Harvard," where a course in law had just been added to the curriculum. Here Norris found a freedom of spirit to his liking, a place where a student could express himself honestly without fear of condemnation. He received his Bachelor of Science degree in 1880, the Bachelor of Laws in 1883, and was admitted to the Indiana bar the same year. Not having the funds to establish a law office he went back to teaching for two years, one of which was spent in Washington Territory. He and his mother talked over the matter of selling out and locating in the far west. It was decided that George should go first and see what it was like. He found the "Promised Land" not so promising. His funds were soon exhausted so he taught awhile and with his earnings bought a ticket as far east as Beatrice, Nebraska, where he hoped to locate. Then he went on to Ohio and taught another term, saved his earnings, borrowed $300 from a sister, and with a deed to 80 acres given him by his mother returned to Beatrice and went into partnership with H. H. Harrington. In less than a year the partnership was dissolved and the young lawyer, now 24, sold his 80 acres in Ohio, moved to Beaver City, bought a quarter section of land and opened an office. His law practice flourished and he became firmly established. He lived in a little room at the rear of his office until, in 1890, he married Pluma Lashley, daughter of a miller and banker. Four children were born to this union, a boy who died at birth and three girls. The family moved to McCook in 1899 and Mrs. Norris died there in 1901 when the third daughter was born. Two years later he married Ellie Leonard, a teacher in McCook, who proved to be a real mother to his children.

Norris' first public office was that of county attorney and he made an excellent record. From 1895 to 1902 he was judge of the 14th district. He liked the work and in later years wondered if he made a mistake in leaving it. These years on the bench broadened his sympathies and strengthened his conception of justice. His decision to run for Congress in 1902 was a momentous one. Little did this quiet and unassuming 41-year-old judge realize that he would spend the next 40 years in that lawmaking body, five terms in the House and five in the Senate. Only in his last term was he officially listed as an Independent but he might as well have carried that label from the start. He served during the administrations of Theodore Roosevelt, Taft, Wilson, Harding, Coolidge, Hoover and Franklin D. Roosevelt. America was emerging as a world power. Great issues were at stake both at home and abroad. The horse and buggy days were giving way to the machine age and the machine age was about to submerge the old principles of our Democracy. The "upper dogs" were putting the squeeze on the "underdogs." Norris more than kept pace with the changing times and from the beginning resolutely championed the cause of the underprivileged.

It would be foolhardy to attempt even a brief run-down on his political career in these few pages. A thumbnail sketch will have to suffice. Norris was first, last and always the Progressive, a thorn in the flesh of professional politicians of both major parties. He followed his conscience and the best line of reasoning he could muster. He fought high tariffs which his own Republican party favored, led the fight to democratize the House of Representatives by taking from a Republican Speaker his dictatorial powers and struck hard against the spoils system. He supported Wilson's reform legislation for tax, tariff, money and banking reforms as well as more stringent laws to curb the trusts. Though he voted against our entering World War I, Norris supported the war to the utmost. Efforts to tack a "pro-German" label on him gave him some unhappy moments, but the people of Nebraska remained loyal to him and he was re-elected shortly after the Armistice was signed.

Fully five years before World War I Norris had advocated a league of nations but voted against *the League* because of commitments involved. On the defensive during the Republican "hay-ride" of the Twenties he, nevertheless, battled for farm relief, rights of labor, conservation, public ownership of hydroelectric power, and the election of presidents by direct vote of the people. He supported Al Smith in 1928 and Franklin D. Roosevelt in 1932 and after. During the Thirties he witnessed many triumphs. The Norris-LaGuardia Act of 1932 restricted the use of injunctions in labor disputes and outlawed the "yellow dog" contract and guaranteed the right of labor to organize and bargain collectively. Almost single-handed he drove through the 20th ("Lame Duck") amendment. The Tennessee Valley Authority Act was the culmination of a long struggle on his part. The Rural Electrification Act was largely the result of his efforts and gave him much satisfaction. He took time out in 1934 to campaign for the establishment of the unicameral legislative system in Nebraska believing it would promote efficiency and economy. Undoubtedly it was through his leadership that the constitutional amendment was approved by the electorate.

Norris announced his plans to retire in 1936 and did not file in the primaries. However, he was persuaded to run as an Independent and was elected by a plurality of some 35,000 votes. His defeat in 1942 was generally attributed to an anti-Roosevelt vote rather than the strength of his opposition. Another world war had come and up to the end of his service in Washington, Norris supported the Administration on every measure and was especially pleased with the Lend-Lease Act as an aid to victory. He voted for price controls and rationing and believed increased taxation necessary to curb inflation. Roosevelt said that Senator Norris was one of the few older statesmen who "preserved the aspirations of youth as they accumulated the wisdom of years."

Senator and Mrs. Norris returned to the quiet of their Mc-Cook home in 1943 where he worked on his autobiography, received many old friends, and took care of his heavy correspondence. The end of a long and rigorous life was not far away. He passed away on September 2, 1944. George Norris was not a member of any church. He said: "I hope that I may be given the humble privilege of being classed as one of the followers of the religion proclaimed by Abou Ben Adhem who remarked to an angel in the night, 'I pray thee, then, write me as one that loves his fellow men.'" And this Gentle Knight did love his fellow men. His whole record is an open book to that effect.

WILLIAM A. PAXTON

Entrepreneur

JANUARY 26, 1837 · JULY 18, 1907

———◆———

"P. & G." is a familiar trademark throughout the nation and is generally considered the label of Procter and Gamble. But, in Omaha's trade territory "P. & G." has long stood for the products of Paxton and Gallagher, two enterprising businessmen of that city. We are concerned here with the first of these men, William A. Paxton, and his "rags to riches" career. His long-time secretary and business manager, B. J. Scannell makes this appraisal: "W. A. Paxton was a wonderful man, in my estimation the greatest builder of Omaha that has ever lived . . . and he has his name associated with more business and commercial enterprises today in Omaha than any other man, living or dead. He brought to Omaha the Union Stock Yards Company which, next to the location of the Union Pacific Railroad Company, was the greatest that Omaha has ever had."

Paxton's name is found in many places. A town, a hotel, a city block, and various commercial enterprises, to say nothing of a great variety of products, bear the name of Paxton. His experiences include that of farmer, foreman, freighter, manager, contractor, cattleman, promoter, speculator, jobber, manufacturer, realtor, executive, and even politician. But, along with his many occupational and business interests, Paxton was always the social-minded citizen. He contributed generously to any forward looking program designed to make Omaha a better place to live. He was every inch a builder. Having experienced both sides of the operation, having been bossed as well as being the boss, Paxton knew the problems of both labor and capital. Hence, he had an understanding mutually advantageous to employee and employer. He was fair-minded, honest, and appreciated a job well done. During his early years he had to scrabble to earn a livelihood. He must have been tempted to join with other young adventurers of his day in the quest for quick wealth in the gold fields of the West. Perhaps he reasoned that "gold is where you find it." At any rate, Paxton chose to find his gold in Nebraska.

William A. Paxton came from Scotch ancestry on his father's side which may partially explain his thrifty habits. He was born on a farm near Springfield, Kentucky, January 26, 1837. William was next to the eldest of five children and his formal education was limited to a few terms at the district school. When he was twelve the family moved to Missouri, settling on a farm near Middleton in Montgomery county. The next year William hired out to a farmer nearby and worked for him a year and a half at $8.50 a month. With his savings he bought ox teams and broke prairie sod for the settlers over a period of two years. Then, for the next four years he managed a farm for M. J. Regan at a salary of $200 a year. Paxton was now almost twenty. He had gained much practical experience and had learned the value of money though possessing very little of it.

At this time Regan, his boss, secured a bridge contract on the old military road between Omaha and Fort Kearny and hired young Paxton as foreman on the project. The two arrived in Omaha, January 13, 1857, and completed the job in December. William then returned to Missouri and, on February 22, 1858, married Mary Jane Ware, who deserves much credit for the remarkable career of her husband. The young couple tried farming for the next two years but with poor success. Hoping to get a "stake" Paxton returned to Omaha in 1860 and this time tried his luck at freighting between Omaha and Denver. This occupation proved to be both arduous and dangerous. The Indians were not exactly friendly on the plains at this time. Again, in 1861, Paxton came into the employ of Regan who was helping build the Western Union telegraph line westward. His pay was now $40 a month. Near the end of the year he returned to Missouri and once more turned to farming, but with the same results as previously. He managed to scrape up $135 and, with his wife, once more headed for Omaha, arriving July 7, 1863.

Paxton was now through with Missouri farming and determined to stake his future in Nebraska. Starting from "scratch" was not easy, he needed a job and was in no position to be "choosy." For almost a year he worked in a livery stable at $50 a month and then was hired to take over a freighting outfit operating between Omaha and Denver and Fort Laramie. Freighting occupied his time until 1867 but he was not content to continue working for others. He bought a team from Edward Creighton for $1,050, on credit, agreeing to pay for it in four months. His optimism was well placed. He built up his business, adding new equipment as his earnings increased.

Now Paxton switched to grading railroad right-of-ways for which there was a great demand. His first contract was a ten-mile stretch west of Julesburg, Colorado, for the Union Pacific. Then he was employed as a foreman by the same road to get out railroad ties. Recognizing his ability to handle men and material he was assigned, June, 1868, to move 6,000 men, 1,500 teams and much equipment of the Union Pacific grading forces from Rock Creek, Wyoming, to Green River in the same territory. He managed this gang for three months and then was sent to Tie Siding, Wyoming, to get out ties once more. That winter he sold his own outfit and returned to Omaha $15,000 richer for his railroad work.

Paxton was now in a position financially to carry out a cherished desire. In May, 1869, he bought a herd of range cattle in Kansas and drove them from Abilene to Omaha. He netted $12,000 on the transaction giving him sufficient capital for further investments. However, he was not yet ended with railroad building. He took a contract to build ten miles of the Omaha and Northwestern Railroad running north from Omaha. He was one of the incorporators of this line and held one-tenth of the stock. Later this road became a part of the Chicago, St. Paul,

Minneapolis and Omaha Railroad. In 1870, Paxton and two other men, secured a five-year contract to supply the Indian agencies with beef. They furnished from 23,000 to 75,000 head of cattle annually and made themselves a very neat profit.

Funds were now available to play the role of a big operator and Paxton had clearly conceived plans to put his money to work. Even before the beef contract expired he had established one of the finest cattle ranches in Nebraska near Ogallala. This ranch was the forerunner of the cattle raising industry in the western part of the state. In the fall of 1883 he sold about 20,000 head of cattle from his ranch to the Ogallala Land and Cattle Company (in which he owned $125,000 worth of stock) for $675,000 and still had 22,000 head left. Twenty years previously Paxton had arrived in Omaha almost "dead broke." He served as president and manager of the above company for several years. He also had ranches near Hyannis and Paxton, Nebraska, the latter town being named in his honor. An old pioneer cowboy, E. A. Hall, who once worked for the Ogallala Land and Cattle Company, remarked recently: "W. A. Paxton was a fine employer. When he came to a cow camp, he'd be in the middle of the men, visiting and joking when the work was done."

After 1875 Paxton seems to have had his hand in about every big commercial venture launched in Omaha. While engaged in the ranch cattle business he sensed the possibilities of Omaha as a packing house center, an outlet for range herds. In 1878 he took the lead in organizing the first Union Stock Yards Company. Operations were carried on in Omaha for awhile, then the company moved to Council Bluffs. The decision to move back to Nebraska and establish the Union Stock Yards Company of South Omaha was a vital one for the future of Omaha and Paxton deserves chief credit for that action. He was intimate with Philip D. Armour and other pioneers of the packing industry who gave him timely advice. All through the remainder of his life Paxton took a leading part in the affairs of the extremely successful Union Stock Yards Company. Not only did he serve as its president but he helped to organize and manage several of its auxiliary agencies. These included the Union Stock Yards Bank of South Omaha, the Union Stock Yards Railroad Company, and the South Omaha Land Syndicate which founded the city of South Omaha.

Paxton was not one to put all his "eggs in one basket." Once on his way he placed his "bets" on several enterprises but it seems that everything he touched was successful. In 1879 he and Ben Gallagher established the wholesale house of Paxton and Gallagher. This company grew into a concern that did much to promote Omaha's jobbing interests. That same year saw the Nebraska Telephone Company organized and Paxton was one of the principal stockholders. The following year he and nine others purchased and equipped the old fair grounds north of Omaha and the state fair was held there for several years. In 1886 the Paxton and Vierling Iron Works was incorporated and through the years has furnished employment for a large number of men. Paxton served as head of the company. He was also president of the Union Elevator Company and of the Union Trust Company. His life had become a busy one, indeed.

Real estate was not the least of Paxton's interests and he accumulated a great deal of it. He was the driving force behind many building programs, directly or indirectly. He is credited with erecting buildings in Omaha that cost more than $600,000 and on this note alone is worthy of the title of "Builder." The Paxton, Ware, and Granite blocks, and the Mercantile Hotel are evidences of his building operations. The Paxton Hotel was named in his honor over his protests. The builders had decided to stop at the fourth floor but Paxton offered to raise the necessary funds to make it five stories. This was done and he, personally, contributed $5,000 toward the edifice.

William A. Paxton affiliated with the Democratic party but could not go along with W. J. Bryan on the free silver question. Like J. Sterling Morton he was a "hard money" advocate. However, he had little time or desire to engage in politics. His only fling was in 1881 when he was elected to the Nebraska House of Representatives. As a power in the business life of Omaha he had few equals. He was in a position to "make or break" many commercial projects. Paxton chose to boost any worthy enterprise but was not easily taken in by "fly by night" promoters. He came up the "hard" way and recognized the full value of a dollar. He possessed keen business judgment and was not carried away by wild, get-rich-quick schemes. But, with all his business acumen, Paxton was always "esteemed as a man of marked generous impulses, and many of his fellow townsmen recall his acts of kindness in lending substantial aid at times when it was most needed." His optimistic faith went far in making Omaha the "Gateway to the West."

JOHN JOSEPH PERSHING

Black Jack

SEPTEMBER 13, 1860 · JULY 15, 1948

IT MAY SEEM a bit presumptuous to claim General Pershing as a Nebraskan as he lived in the state only four years except for frequent visits. But his intentions were good. He bought a home in Lincoln in 1920 where he planned to live on his retirement. However, his work in connection with the American Memorial Cemetery in France and other assignments kept him too busy. Then, because of serious illness and advancing age, he lived in seclusion at Walter Reed Hospital in Washington the last seven years of his life. Ever since he instructed university cadets at Lincoln, 1891–1895, under the title of Professor of Military Science and Tactics, Nebraskans have felt that he belongs to them a little bit more than to any other state. The Pershing Rifles, which he organized, and the Pershing Medal, awarded to the top man in that company each year, help to keep his mem-

[147]

ory green. He, also, earned a law degree while there and was admitted to the Nebraska bar. His sisters lived in Lincoln and the General dropped in for visits whenever feasible. Once when visiting in Omaha he said: "I am proud to call Nebraska my home," and another time remarked that "Omaha has more patriotism to the square inch than any other city I have ever visited." Missourians may dispute Nebraska's claim but the claim will, nevertheless, be made. It matters little anyhow, for he is big enough for both.

Pershing's life is one of many triumphs and deep tragedy. His span of years include the Civil War, Indian Wars, Spanish-American War, Philippine Insurrection, Mexican Border Affair, World War I, and World War II. In all but the first and last he was an active participant. His great tragedy occurred in 1915 when he lost his wife and three daughters in a fire that destroyed the Pershing home in San Francisco. Only his son, Warren, was saved. Perhaps, no one in our history has had more military assignments and more military responsibilities than General John Joseph Pershing. Dr. Fred Morrow Fling, eminent historian at the University of Nebraska for many years, made these comments in 1931 when Pershing was awarded the distinguished service medal by the Lincoln Kiwanis Club:

"He possessed in those days (1891–95) all the fine soldierly characteristics that distinguished him as commander of the American armies in France. He had a fine presence, a genial and unpretentious manner and one gained the impression that he was a man of great physical reserve coupled with unusual driving power. His speech was incisive; he was quick in decision and quick in action."

Dr. Fling's estimate would apply at any time in the life of Pershing. He was "every inch a soldier" who followed the military code to the letter and expected those under his command to do the same. A stickler for details, he wanted his men to know that the little things count even to the buttons on the uniform. An officer in the A. E. F. writing in 1921 said:

"In France and since he came home he has kept his head, he has not been indiscreet in any small particular. He has not talked. He has not gone out of his way to seek popular applause. He has not tried to make occasion for ovations. He has spoken only when asked to speak, and when he has said anything he has confined himself to the business in hand. The armies in France did not idolize or idealize him. They did not bring him home as a great popular hero.

They did not want him as a candidate for President. But this attitude of indifference was not confined to General Pershing; it extended to all the other commanding generals of our forces in France. The great bulk of the men who went over were glad enough to be through with military ways and professional military men when the end came. I think they gave General Pershing full credit for everything he did in France. I think the common feeling among them was and is that he did his part well as he knew how, and they did theirs in the same fashion."

Perhaps his men had a feeling that he was "breathing down their necks" and that it was a sign of bad luck to cross the path of the "Old Man." Yet, most all agreed that he was the right man to run the show.

Pershing's great-great grandfather Frederick came from Alsace, France, in 1794 and the name then was Pfershing. John Joseph, son of John Fletcher and Ann Elizabeth Thompson Pershing, was born in a railroad house in Meadville, Missouri, September 13, 1860. His father was a section boss of a seven mile stretch on the old Hannibal and St. Louis railway. Johnny was the oldest of nine children. He spent his youth on a farm, attended the local school and qualified as a teacher. He then taught at Laclede and Prairie Mound saving enough money to attend college at Kirksville Normal, graduating from there with a Bachelor of Arts degree in 1880. His father abandoned his railroad job and followed other pursuits such as operating a hotel, a store and postoffice and even tried his luck as a traveling salesman. An unfortunate land investment wiped out his holdings; hence young John and the others had to earn their own ways.

Two years following his graduation John read a newspaper story telling about examinations for West Point Military Academy. He won admission over 16 competitors and four years later, 1886, graduated with highest honors, was president of his class and received his commission as a second lieutenant. The farm boy from Missouri was doing all right. His first assignment was with the 6th Cavalry in New Mexico where he served under Nelson A. Miles scouting renegade Apaches of Geronimo. During the winter of 1890–91 he was with his regiment in South Dakota participating in the roundup of rebellious Sioux that culminated in the battle of Wounded Knee. These experiences gave him the training needed in later operations in the Philippines and Mexico. The next four years, spent at the University of Nebraska, were rather pleasant ones and probably gave him a desire to some day make Lincoln his permanent home. He did a remarkable job of revamping the cadet organization. Dr. Fling remarks: "Only those who know what the state of the military department was when he took command and what it was when he left the University . . . can realize what he accomplished in the face of a hostile public opinion on the part of many of the faculty and students."

After leaving the University he was attached to the 10th Cavalry, a Negro unit. It was at this time he won the nickname "Black Jack." He was in charge of the roundup of Cree Indians in the Northwest and these were deported to Canada after which he did a turn in instructing at the United States Military Academy. The Spanish-American War had started and, rejoining his regiment, he took part in the Cuban campaign winning high praise for bravery in the fighting around San Juan. At the War's end he was given the task of organizing the War Department's Bureau of Insular Affairs and served as Chief the following year. He detested departmental duties and he managed to wangle an assignment to the Philippines where an insurrection of the natives was in full swing.

Between 1899 and 1913 most of Pershing's service was in the Philippines where he won outstanding praise, especially in the campaigns against the rugged Moros. However, 1905–1906, he was military attache at Tokyo and a military observer with Kuroki's army in Manchuria during the Russo-Japanese War, and served on the General Staff at Washington for awhile. He was commissioned a captain in the cavalry in 1901 and in 1905 President Theodore Roosevelt jumped him to brigadier general over 862 senior officers. There was an outcry, some claiming the advancement was due to the influence of Pershing's father-in-law, Senator Francis E. Warren of Wyoming. Subsequent events proved it was a well-deserved promotion. In the Philippines he held various administrative posts but most of the time was active in field operations. He was specially cited for unusual acts of bravery in the Battle of Mt. Bagsak, June 12, 1913, where he directed the fighting at a critical stage and defeated a group of die-hard fanatical Moros. Pershing was always tactful in his dealings with the natives and exerted every effort to make friends with them. "He maintained contact with people of an alien race without friction, studied their dialects, customs and religion, and established friendly intercourse with the native chiefs, receiving them in camp and visiting them in return."

After completing his service in the Philippines in the fall of 1913 he was in command of the 8th Cavalry Brigade at the Presidio in San Francisco. But he was not destined to remain here long as trouble was brewing on the Mexican border. Mexican bandits were making depredations and these reached a climax when a force, led by Francisco Villa, made a raid on the town of Columbus, New Mexico, March 9, 1916. Pershing was ordered by President Wilson to lead an expedition of 20,000 into Mexico to capture the bandit leader and stop these forays. Mexico was torn by civil strife and the Carranza government, while agreeing to the move, used obstruction tactics against Pershing's forces. The Mexican people resented the presence of foreign troops on their soil. He was finally ordered to withdraw his troops and the crossing into Texas was made February 5, 1917. Villa was still at large. During these operations Pershing had been advanced to major general.

Events in Europe were overshadowing the Mexican imbroglio. War had been raging there since 1914 and we entered the conflict April 6, 1917. On May 19, Black Jack was selected to command the American Expeditionary Forces. Again there was furor for passing him over other men. Sailing secretly he and his small force arrived in Paris, June 13, amid a tumultuous welcome. Almost immediately Pershing became involved in a hot dispute with Allied commanders who wanted to use American troops as reinforcements for the British and French. The General remained adamant and refused to let his troops lose their identity. Wilson backed him on this stand and though Americans were used at various places to "block the holes," in the main they fought on their own sectors under their own officers as an independent army. Pershing was made "General of the Armies of the U. S." by act of Congress, 1919.

The story of the War cannot be told here but Dr. Fling makes this concise summarization relative to Pershing's leadership in it.

"In less than forty years, General Pershing had scaled the military ladder from its lowest to its highest rung. At every stage of his progress he had justified the confidence of those who, in the early days, believed that he would go far if the opportunity arose, but until 1917, none of the tasks that fell to him was big enough to give a real measure of the man. When he was given command of the American troops sent to France, we realized that the big opportunity, the full test of his powers had come. . . . The task he had accepted was one to make the boldest hesitate. He had not simply

[151]

to command an army, but to create one in the face of the enemy and struggling against the efforts of the allies to employ the American levies as replacement troops for their constantly dwindling armies . . . Never in human history had any people undertaken so gigantic a task as America undertook . . . nor accomplished it in so short a time. There was . . . no time to lose. The chances seemed to be that Germany would win the war before America could bring her mighty strength to bear. To create so vast an army (4,000,000), to transport it to Europe over an ocean strewn with mines and haunted by submarines, to feed it on the other side, to whip it in shape, and to get it into the trenches seemed an undertaking too great for human strength. But America accomplished the impossible. When the great drive began in the summer of 1918, the First American Army occupied the most difficult sector on the allied front, that of the Argonne . . . Sweeping through the famous St. Mihiel salient the Germans had held since the beginning of the war, and up through the Argonne the American army cut the German line and the war was practically over.

"It was, indeed, a distinguished service that General Pershing had given to his country and to the cause of civilization, in a struggle 'to make the world safe for democracy.' He had shown that he possessed the abilities of a great organizer, and a great leader. And through it all, he kept his head."

The General was greatly disappointed in the terms of the armistice. He believed the only way to stamp out Prussian militarism was to move into Berlin. But he was overruled. On his 85th birthday, 1945, President Truman sent him this message: "This should be one of the happiest of your many birthdays as you remember that this time we went all the way to Berlin, as you counselled in 1918."

Pershing attended the Peace Conference and helped in framing the military terms and returned to the United States September 8, 1919. He was made Chief of Staff in 1921 and set to work reorganizing the army, a difficult task as popular sentiment was opposed to a large force in peacetime. These were the "Roaring Twenties" and the people wanted to live "high wide and handsome." Nevertheless, Pershing did an admirable job of co-ordinating the regular service, national guard, and the organized reserves. If his recommendations had been followed more closely we might have averted World War II. On reaching the age limit, September 13, 1924, he retired from the Army but continued to accept special assignments and offer advice when requested. He was one of three official delegates appointed by

Franklin D. Roosevelt to attend the coronation of George VI. In spite of his poor state of health he addressed the Nation by radio in 1940 warning the people of the seriousness of the world situation.

Honors have been heaped upon General Pershing such as never accorded an American soldier. His foreign decorations make up a long list. He declined the Distinguished Service Cross following World War I but President Franklin D. Roosevelt presented it to him on his 80th birthday for "a dangerous charge he had led against the Moros in the Philippine Islands." At the age of 87 Congress authorized a special gold medal "in recognition of his fearless leadership, heroic achievements and great military victories," and the Army and Navy Union awarded him a medal for "a life of outstanding service to the country." Honorary degrees were conferred by the University of Nebraska, 1917; St. Andrews of Scotland, 1919; Oxford and Cambridge, 1919; Yale, 1920; Pennsylvania Military Academy, 1921. He was a 33rd degree Mason and belonged to several military clubs. After his retirement he set to work on a book, *My Experiences in the World War*, which was published in 1931. He passed away in Washington, July 15, 1948. Honors continue to be bestowed upon him. In 1953 the new armory on the University of Nebraska College of Agriculture campus was named the Pershing Memorial Armory.

General Pershing was not only every inch a soldier, but every inch a man, "generous, warm-hearted, genial, frank and unassuming, the finest type of an American." Nebraskans proudly claim him as one of their own.

LOUISE POUND

Scholar

JUNE 30, 1872

IN NEBRASKA, when one mentions the name "Pound" it is not
likely to be the famous jurist who comes to mind but rather his
famous sisters, Louise and Olivia. Dean Roscoe Pound used to
jokingly remark that in Nebraska circles he is known as "Louise
Pound's brother." This is no reflection on Nebraskans or Dean
Pound, for his greatness has been achieved more outside the
state while Louise has kept her feet on Nebraska soil. In her
"ivy tower" at the University of Nebraska, Louise Pound has
made a name for herself, brought distinction to that center of
learning, and prestige to the state. Olivia, while not receiving
the acclaim of her brilliant sister, has touched the lives of thousands of students at Lincoln High School and kept alive, on the
secondary educational level, a love for the classics. The Pound
family has probably contributed more culturally to the Univer-

[154]

sity of Nebraska than any other group. Perhaps some day a building will be erected on the campus as a memorial to this illustrious trio. If so, it would be a well-deserved tribute.

Back at the turn of the century Louise Pound was "burning up the tennis courts" throughout the midwest and collecting an assortment of titles. Even while working for a doctor's degree in Heidelberg, Germany, she brought out her racquet, won the women's singles, and with her male partner, the mixed doubles championships. She was ready to challenge the men as well as the women. In 1891 she won the men's tennis championship at the University of Nebraska and the next year, with Emory Hardy, the men's doubles. This was only a starter. She carried away the women's state championship in 1891 and 1892 and the Western championship in Chicago in 1897. She and Guy "Rolling Along" Williams teamed up to win the men's doubles in Lincoln in 1900. In 1903, she and Carrie Neeley "took" the Central Western doubles and in 1915 the women's Western doubles at Kansas City, and Lake Forest, Illinois.

But, Louise's athletic prowess was not confined to tennis. She took up other outdoor sports and held her own in rugged competition. Golf was considered a "sissy" game in the midwest but there was nothing mild about the way this young lady performed on the fairways. She was the ranking woman golfer of Lincoln from 1902 until 1928, and won the state championship in 1916. During the Nineties and early Nineteen-Hundreds cycling was an extremely popular sport, and Louise took to it "like a duck takes to water." She joined the Century Road Club of America and in 1896 won the Rainbow Gold Medal for wheeling five thousand miles. An expert ice skater, she excelled in figure skating and together with another enthusiast introduced skiing to the Lincoln area. Basketball was a new sport but a team of "bloomer girls" was organized at the University that played other universities and colleges. The trainer and manager was none other than Miss Pound.

It is often said that education and athletics do not mix. Louise Pound gives the lie to this statement. Though sports were not so highly organized and ballyhooed as now, nevertheless, the participants played for "keeps" even though few spectators were on hand to cheer. Miss Pound has always given her best whether on the playing field, in the classroom, writing a magazine article or book, working on a committee, or helping with some civic enterprise.

Louise Pound was born in Lincoln on June 30, 1872, five years after Nebraska got its "wings." Her father, Stephen Bosworth Pound, was just getting established in the legal profession. Her mother, Laura Biddlecombe Pound, an unusually intelligent and resourceful woman, was responsible for the early education of Louise and her brother and sister. The results prove she did a splendid job. Mrs. Pound had little confidence in the public schools of early Lincoln. The Pound home was a model of regularity but the schedule included time for social activities. Here the younger set gathered for many good times. The home, in those Victorian days, was the recreational center and that of Stephen Pound was an unusually popular place.

Louise's higher education at the state university proceeded according to plan. Her high scholastic average brought the coveted Phi Beta Kappa key. She received a bachelor's degree in 1892 and her master's in 1895. Along with her regular academic work she studied music and earned a diploma in that field. In addition, she served as a teaching fellow for three years getting a taste of the other side of the classroom. The summers of 1897 and 1898 were spent at the University of Chicago where she took special courses and was initiated into the wonders of the big city. Between 1897 and 1899, Louise was a regular instructor on the Nebraska faculty. Realizing the need of a doctor's degree to advance herself in the teaching and writing fields, she went abroad to study and received the degree of Doctor of Philosophy from Heidelberg University in 1900. A half-century ago a degree from a German university was considered the ultimate in higher education. Apparently, Miss Pound had "arrived." Returning to Nebraska she took up where she left off at the University, now as adjunct professor. Since that date in 1900 Miss Pound has advanced steadily, first to assistant professor, then associate professor and in 1912, full professor, a position held until her retirement in 1945 when she was given emeritus standing.

Louise Pound had received a most thorough education. She specialized in literature and languages and is rated one of the leading literary critics. But, unlike many scholars, she has found time for many activities outside the classroom and her study. While a student, and all through her career as a teacher, she has helped with the University extra-curricular program. Projects like *The Sombrero* and *The Cornhusker*, student yearbooks, were improved greatly by her assistance. Her interest in sports, already mentioned, did not wane. Here is a well-rounded personality who loves life and has put much into making her environment a better one. While some of her colleagues grouched about trivial matters, Dr. Pound looked upon the bright side of things and went about her daily work with a spirit of optimism and faith in the future.

Folklore has ever been a subject of interest to Dr. Pound and to this day she maintains that interest. Only recently she contributed an article to *Nebraska History* on "The John G. Maher Hoaxes." She is a member of the American Folklore Society and was its president from 1924 to 1926. Membership is likewise held in the American Dialect Society, and the National Folk Festival Society and she edited the magazine *Folksay,* 1929–1930. Her book, *Poetic Origins and the Ballad,* published in 1922, was followed the next year by *American Ballads and Songs.* In addition to her books she has written many articles on the ballad. A collection of her works, *Selected Writings of Louise Pound,* came from the press in 1949.

Dr. Pound, though a specialist in her field, has always maintained an interest in and close connection with, the whole field of education. She has served on various committees and has appeared on programs of such organizations as the State Teachers' Association, Nebraska Academy of Science, the American Association of University Professors and the Daughters of the American Revolution. During the First World War she was a member of the Belgian Relief Committee, headed a group that sent a large shipment of soap to the French peasants, and took an active part in the work of the National League of Women's Service. Dr. Pound might be called a "joiner" but with this difference. When she joins an organization she does so with the idea of putting something into it as well as getting something out of it, and she usually does both. A complete list of her affiliations cannot be set down here, but some not already mentioned are: International Phonetic, Modern Language, and Humanistic Research associations; the Medieval Academy; National Council of English Teachers; Nebraska Writers' Guild; and the American Association of University Women. These and other organizations are proud to have her as a member. Her advice and constructive criticism is eagerly sought and her book reviews are widely read.

She has contributed many articles on a variety of subjects in both the English and American fields of literature. These are too numerous to list here but are the results of intensive research in many periods in the development of the English language. She has delved into the origins and evolution of words with noteworthy success. Two of her books in this field are: *Comparison of Adjectives in English in the Fifteenth and Sixteenth Centuries;* and *Blends, Their Relation to English Word Formation.* While finding time in her busy teaching schedule for writing and serving on editorial and advisory boards, she has, somehow, managed to get away and give lectures at several universities, including the Universities of California, Chicago, Yale, Columbia, and Stanford. Smith College conferred the honorary degree of Doctor of Literature on Dr. Pound in 1928. She was awarded the Kiwanis distinguished service medal in 1947 and the Nebraska Alumni Association honored her in a similar manner the next year.

If further proof is necessary to show that Dr. Pound is a versatile "live-wire," these additional academic and social organizations to which she belongs may be cited: Kappa Kappa Gamma, Theta Sigma Phi, Delta Omicron, Delta Kappa Gamma, Chi Delta Phi, Sigma Tau Delta, Alpha Lambda Delta, Pi Gamma Mu, Lincoln Country Club, University Club, Mortar Board, Auto Club, Copper Kettle Club and the Omaha Woman's Press Club. How does she do it? That, is a good question. Most mortals would be dizzy from it all. Not Louise Pound. She loves it and thrives on it. She never married. Perhaps this fact gives part of the answer! Few women, indeed, can begin to match the record of this native daughter of Nebraska. Her life has been a constructive one and her contributions in the academic field are beyond measurement. Let us hope that she will leave an autobiography revealing her impressions of these many years as observed from her ringside seat in the Capital City of Lincoln.

NATHAN ROSCOE POUND

Phenomenal Jurist

OCTOBER 27, 1870

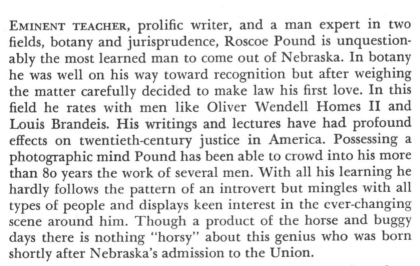

EMINENT TEACHER, prolific writer, and a man expert in two fields, botany and jurisprudence, Roscoe Pound is unquestionably the most learned man to come out of Nebraska. In botany he was well on his way toward recognition but after weighing the matter carefully decided to make law his first love. In this field he rates with men like Oliver Wendell Homes II and Louis Brandeis. His writings and lectures have had profound effects on twentieth-century justice in America. Possessing a photographic mind Pound has been able to crowd into his more than 80 years the work of several men. With all his learning he hardly follows the pattern of an introvert but mingles with all types of people and displays keen interest in the ever-changing scene around him. Though a product of the horse and buggy days there is nothing "horsy" about this genius who was born shortly after Nebraska's admission to the Union.

Returning from an out-of-town football game where he had helped with the cheer-leading, Roscoe reported: "It was a glorious victory and I got home from Omaha speechless and dead broke." He found the game a stimulating outlet. In fact he "became a football nut," to the extent that he wrote a short history of the sport. He even wrote songs and yells, some in Latin, and did some officiating. Pound, also, interested himself in military science and other subjects. With sparkling eyes he kept his classes in good humor and alert to the subject in hand. He remembered the names of the law students, even those not in his classes, and in later years loved to stand around at bar association gatherings and greet them by name.

Roscoe's father, Stephen Pound, migrated to Lincoln in 1866 where he opened a small merchandising shop while studying Nebraska law. Later, in 1868, he was one of the first six lawyers admitted to the bar in Lincoln. The next year he went east for his bride, Laura Biddlecombe. He was regarded highly as a lawyer and from 1875 to 1887 served as a district judge. Roscoe's mother was an exceptional woman and not being satisfied with the public schools of Lincoln took it upon herself to teach her children. She discovered early that Roscoe had a wonderful memory and this was the key to his rapid progress. He once wrote: "The secret of my success is my blame memory." A case of measles had left him with weak eyes. This handicap, however, seemed only to sharpen his intellect. He entered the university at the age of 14 having spent two years in the preparatory school there. His chief interest was botany, a field in which his parents lent encouragement. At home he had been supplied with cabinets, setting boards and other paraphernalia and had a large collection of insects properly mounted and classified. In the university he studied under the celebrated Dr. Charles E. Bessey and following his graduation in 1888 continued on, working for a master's degree. Bessey put him in charge of the laboratory at a yearly salary of six hundred dollars. As an undergraduate Pound had also majored in the classics, having mastered Latin and Greek with ease. These subjects stood him in well when he later entered the field of law.

Having earned his Master of Arts degree in botany he set out in the fall of 1889 for Harvard. The man he had hoped to study under, Asa Gray, died the previous year and his successors seemed to have little to offer that Roscoe had not already learned under Bessey. So, at this point, he decided to study law.

He spent this year at Harvard in the role of a "grind" for he was there to learn whereas most of the college set were more interested in a good time. While in Boston he did take advantage of the culture there, going on excursion trips, to the theatre and to the opera. He was a great lover of music. His next move was back to Lincoln and the practice of law. However, he still had his yearning for the study of plant life and completed the requirements for a Ph.D. in that field in 1897.

Though his major contributions are in law, Pound's influence in the botanical field is of no small consequence. He and Dr. F. E. Clements made a survey of plant life in Nebraska and effected changes in the system of classification, fitting it more to the needs of this and other states and getting away somewhat from the German ecology. Subsequent works in ecology or phytogeography are greatly indebted to their studies. Pound's botanical efforts did much to simplify and clarify the nomenclature as well as avoid much duplication in terminology. He is listed in *American Men of Science* as a phytogeographer among the 100 top men in the field of botany, and as one of the thousand leading American scientists.

But Roscoe Pound is seldom referred to as a scientist. Jurisprudence is his forte. After his year at Harvard he opened an office in Lincoln and soon gained the respect of the legal fraternity. While practicing he also taught law at the university until 1907 and served as dean of the Law School from 1903 to 1907. His services were in great demand as shown by the honors that came to him. He was secretary of the Nebraska State Bar Association from 1901 to 1907, Commissioner of Uniform Laws of Nebraska from 1904 to 1907, Commissioner of Appeals on the Supreme Court of Nebraska from 1901 to 1903, and while serving in this latter capacity took no salary from the university. The early years of his career, spent in Lincoln, witnessed much political upheaval. Pound was not a joiner of crusades and kept within the fold of the Republican party. Yet he "sharply rebuked industrialists because he resented their smug complacence with conditions which gave them large profits." He took an active part in local politics, holding offices within the party, but never aspired to public office for the law held too much fascination for him.

He married Grace Gerrard of Columbus, Nebraska, and they were ideally suited having many common interests. She encouraged him in his work and made the Pound home an ideal place for a student of the law. He was active in the Masonic Lodge and in 1915 published a book, *Philosophy of Freemasonry*, in which he set forth in four lectures the teachings of early Masonic notables and concluded with the philosophy of twentieth century Masonry.

Pound's reputation was beginning to extend beyond Nebraska. He was invited to address the spring meeting of the American Bar Association in 1906, the first instance of a law teacher speaking before that group. This young man of 35 set the delegates back on their heels. Instead of the usual "sober, solid, exposition" usually heard he proceeded to point out the weaknesses of our judicial system. "Our system of courts is archaic. Our procedure is behind the times. Our judicial power is wasted. The worst feature of procedure is the lavish granting of new trials. The court's time is frittered away on mere points of legal etiquette. Our legislation is crude. Putting courts in politics has almost destroyed the traditional respect for the Bench." In short, the Dean gave them the "works." Such an outburst from a young Westerner was distressing indeed to the old guard, and they fussed and fumed. But many young men in the association were pleased and heartened. Before the year's end Dean Wigmore of Northwestern had invited Pound to his staff, much to the disappointment of Nebraskans. Wigmore lost him to the University of Chicago two years later but his stay there was short. An article by the professor had come to the attention of Dean Ezra Thayer of Harvard and it convinced him that Pound was the man for the Story professorship in that institution. It was a wise choice for Harvard and a happy development for the young genius.

At Harvard Pound, in 1910, began a career that was to be almost unparalleled in the teaching of law in America. He became Dean in 1916, serving in that capacity until 1936 and then continuing as a law professor to 1947. Offers came to him including the presidency of the University of Wisconsin in 1925, but he preferred to teach and write. He loved his work and the environment of Harvard. His students were happy when he turned down offers from other places. As a teacher Pound assumed his students were seeking the truth and he respected their ideas. Hence, he instilled in them a feeling of confidence. He encouraged the formation of law clubs at Harvard and gave of his time generously to make them function. Through these he became acquainted with many students whom otherwise he would not have known since he did not teach a freshman law course. He helped individual students in getting jobs and straightening out their personal affairs. Pound was one of the most approachable men despite his crowded schedule. He and Mrs. Pound found limited time to travel abroad. In 1922 he lectured at several European universities where he was well received. His fame had become world-wide by his writings as well as through his many "disciples."

The writings of Roscoe Pound in the field of jurisprudence make up a long list. Each year brought forth a new contribution, many of these being lectures given at various universities and meetings of the legal fraternity. "Spirit of the Common Law" and "Theory of Social Interests" appeared in 1921, "Introduction to the Philosophy of Law," 1922, "Interpretations of Legal History," 1923, "Law and Morals," 1924, "Criminal Justice in America," 1926. So it went from year to year: "The Formative Era of American Law," 1938, "History and Systems of the Common Law," 1939, "Organization of the Courts," and "Contemporary Justice Theory," 1940. In the latter year he received the gold medal service award of the American Bar Association. His "Appellate Procedure in Civil Cases" appeared in 1941, "Administrative Law, Its Growth, Procedure and Significance," and "Social Control Through Law," in 1942 and "The Task of Law," in 1944. He collaborated with Felix Frankfurter in directing a survey of criminal justice in Cleveland, Ohio. Offered the presidency of the University of Wisconsin in 1925, he refused the invitation after due consideration. Letters poured in from lawyers and former students urging him to stay on at Harvard. He served on President Hoover's Commission on Law Enforcement, 1929–1931. Many honors were heaped upon him. Honorary degrees have been conferred by both American and European universities. Michigan was the first in 1913. Others include Nebraska, Missouri, Brown, Harvard (1920), Cambridge (England), Union, Pittsburgh, Colorado, George Washington, California, Cincinnati, Rutgers, Boston, and Berlin. Roscoe Pound does not hold an "earned" law degree in the ordinary sense yet "he is the world's foremost doctor of laws having doctored the laws of the United States and other Western countries" for more than half a century.

Harvard University Law School established a Roscoe Pound Professorship of Law in 1950. Just prior to this the Nebraska

Bar Association instituted a "Roscoe Pound Memorial Lectureship." These are honors that usually come posthumously but those behind these moves could see no reason for delay. This octogenarian who has contributed so much to the legal fraternity is highly deserving of these honors and more. When Pound "retired" from Harvard in 1947 he traveled to China to serve as adviser to the Ministry of Justice at Nanking. Since then he has been a visiting professor of law at the University of California and has lectured in other places. His mind, seemingly, is as clear as ever. His name has often been mentioned for a place on the Supreme Court but he was too conservative for the New Dealers and too liberal for the Republicans. Perhaps it is better that he remained a teacher and writer, for service on the bench would have limited his contributions in these fields.

Pound's first wife died in 1928 and for three years he was a lonely widower. In 1931 he married Mrs. Lucy Berry Miller and this marriage, also, proved to be a happy one. His biographer Paul Sayre makes this appraisal of the great jurist:

"Many thousand students owe to him much of their personal and professional lives, not only from work in his classes, but also from moot court work in the law clubs and indeed, everywhere in the law school, under the amazing experience of his personal guidances. It is difficult to describe the deep allegiance of respect and affection that his students have for Pound; it is impossible to explain it."

And the late Charles Evans Hughes, former Chief Justice of the Supreme Court, commented:

"Roscoe Pound, by his profound studies and varied activities has a unique place among American scholars. By reason of his wide knowledge of legal subjects and his rare talent for exposition he has been a brilliant teacher. His writings constitute a notable contribution to the science of jurisprudence. He has also been a close student of the practical problems of the courts and has greatly aided in promoting sound administrative measures."

Perhaps his greatest contribution has been changing the accent from analytical jurisprudence (fixed rules) to sociological jurisprudence (social needs). Undoubtedly, Roscoe Pound is the brainiest man to come out of Nebraska.

HENRY FRANK SCHULTE

Coach

FEBRUARY 2, 1878 · OCTOBER 18, 1944

HE WAS NICKNAMED "Indian" in prep school because of his high cheek bones and long, black hair. As he reached middle age his friends added "Pa." Many affectionately referred to him as "The Coach." Whatever moniker might be used he was known over the state as "Nebraska's Grand Old Man." Henry Frank Schulte has had no peer in the annals of Cornhusker coaching. Few, if any, have so vitally affected the lives of so many young men in the state of Nebraska. His influence reached beyond national limits and, like the spirit of Gandhi, continues to penetrate and shape the youth of today in the field of sports. Thousands of coaches who, directly or indirectly, have been fortunate enough to come under his tutelage carry on the program he so ably set in motion.

Schulte's passing from the scene in 1944 took "one of the

most dynamic and picturesque figures in the field of collegiate athletics; but left standing was the monument he had built to high standards of coaching and sportsmanship, clean living, loyalty, hard training, leadership, tenacity, and fair play." Indicative of "Pa" Schulte's philosophy is an inscription on the *Omaha World-Herald* Schulte Memorial Trophy, awarded each year to the winning school in the Big Seven track meet. "Always finish the race; even if you're last, finish." Seldom did his boys finish last, but if they did, that was all right, too. All Schulte expected of a lad was to "give it all he had," but he did expect him to finish the race.

Writing about Schulte's powerful personality, sports writer Floyd Olds says: "When the tanned, husky-voiced coach put his hand on the shoulder of a pupil, the boy forgot all else, and listened. Pa would say in a kind, fatherly voice: 'Son, you have the makings of a great hurdler. Just stretch out and lengthen that stride a bit, and you'll be a champion!' " The tremendous respect held for this great athletic teacher is attested by the dignified attention given him at track meets. "He could hold an entire crowd in his spell, as well as one athlete or one squad. When Schulte held his hand up and walked down in front of the stands at a high school meet, everyone became silent. The Indian would introduce a new record holder—and the spontaneous applause would be as much for Schulte as for the kid."

Henry Frank Schulte was born near St. Louis, Missouri, February 2, 1878, and started his athletic career playing football at Smith Academy in that city. After finishing prep school he enrolled at Washington University in St. Louis and continued to play football. However, he decided to transfer to the University of Michigan where he would have a better opportunity to display his abilities and move in a faster conference. His four-year record on the gridiron was outstanding and he was rated All-American honors as a guard on Fielding Yost's celebrated "point-a-minute" team. Following graduation the Indian published a magazine for two years at Ann Arbor but he got the coaching fever and accepted a position at Cape Girardeau State Teachers College in southeastern Missouri. Here he coached all three major sports and definitely decided that coaching would be his life's work.

After his initial coaching job at Cape Girardeau, Schulte assisted Yost at the University of Michigan the year of 1913. Then he moved on to the University of Missouri as assistant in football and head track coach. Though his own participation had been primarily in football the Indian was destined to make his national reputation as a teacher of track. He began to develop stars who broke former records and it soon became apparent that he had some kind of special "medicine." One of his proteges, Bob Simpson, demonstrated new techniques in hurdling and set new world's records. John P. Nicholson of Olympic fame and later track coach at Notre Dame, was another pupil who carried out his master's methods and philosophy. To even list the champions developed under his guidance would necessitate many pages. Schulte won much acclaim at the University of Missouri as a football and track mentor of high caliber. His teams won Missouri Valley championships in five of the six years he spent coaching there.

He came to the University of Nebraska as head coach in football and track in 1919 following World War I. Football fortunes were at a low ebb there due to the low manpower of 1917 and 1918. There was a fairly good crop of sophomores on the Indian's squad but it takes time to whip a group of young athletes into shape and teach them the fundamentals of the game. His two years as head football coach brought eight victories, six defeats and three ties. Not a bad record in view of the over-all situation, but not up to pre-war standards. Schulte was a genius in handling the line, so when Fred T. Dawson took over the reins of head football coach in 1921 he, wisely, kept the Indian on as line coach. It is very likely Schulte would have presented championship teams had he been retained as head coach. However, patience is a quality most fans do not possess. But, the Missourian had patience and plenty of good sense. Instead of griping, he went about his assignment of developing forward walls and the results proved that he built well.

But football did not get all the spotlight. Track and field athletics began to take on new vigor at the University. The Indian, as head track coach, started a renaissance in this field such as had never been seen in the midlands. And it was not just a "pop-gun" revolution. He lifted track to a major sport and stirred interest in every corner of the state for a quarter of a century. Gifted with a personality unequaled anywhere, Schulte captivated all who knew him and rapidly became a Nebraska institution. Thousands of young men, directly or indirectly, were inspired to develop their physical potentialities through the wizardry of this magician of the track. Here was a sport in which the little fellows could excel as well as the big muscle boys. His product went forth from the University not only well trained for coaching but also indoctrinated with the Schultian psychology for developing better young citizens.

The name "Pa" was becoming more and more appropriate for the graying track pedagogue. Each year he came up with new ideas and innovations, for Schulte was not content to rest on his laurels. He was a continuous student of his specialty and a past master at organization. The National Collegiate Track and Field Meet is largely the result of his thinking and promotional skill. These meets have done much to raise standards and stimulate public interest. Recognizing that track lacked the crowd appeal of most other sports Schulte decided to do something about it. He introduced a number of aids to make it easier for spectators to understand and enjoy what was taking place on the field at track meets. Programs, showing the events, participants and their pictures, records of past performances and other interesting data, were distributed. Bands were on hand to provide glamour to the occasion. Loudspeakers announced the results of each event so that fans could keep "score." The meets were timed to run on schedule so that spectators, if they wished, need not sit through the entire program.

High school track was encouraged by a system of awards sent out from Schulte's office. Thousands of boys were eager to "go out for track" in the hope of winning a "half-blue" or "full blue" numeral. Lads who never dreamed that they "had what it takes" found themselves sporting medals and ribbons. Thus encouraged, many continued their competition in some college or university. The greatest ambition of a high school track star was to "make" Pa Schulte's team. Honor plaques were awarded by the University to those schools whose athletes rated high scholastically. Schulte believed that a good athlete should measure up to his best as a student. He rightly contended that a good athletic program will make for an improved academic one. And there is no better place to learn cooperation than on an athletic field, according to this talented coach.

Schulte's record at the University of Nebraska has few equals. He won the outdoor track championship ten of the twenty years he served as coach. This competition included the Missouri Valley Conference and its worthy successor, the Big Six. He was uncanny at spotting talent, as well as correcting little flaws and bringing his charges to physical peaks at the crucial moment. Somehow he had the knack of getting his proteges to do just a bit better than they were supposed to do. Third and fourth place winners often made the difference in winning a championship. Rival coaches knew they were matching wits with a miracle man and they always had the highest respect for the Old Master.

Schulte's worth was recognized when he was chosen a member of the coaching staff of the American Olympic team in 1928. His special assignment was to work with the decathlon candidates. Following the games at Amsterdam he visited several European countries and discussed training methods and techniques with physical education leaders. His abilities were regarded highly and, on invitation, he returned the next year and lectured in Germany, France, and England. He was a valuable member of the National Collegiate Rules Committee and was responsible for much of the clarification and standardization of the athletic code in the field of track. His advice was often sought and freely given. Wherever track was the theme of the conversation Schulte's name invariably became part of that conversation—and still does.

The Indian loved to talk track at any time or place. His enthusiasm provoked much discussion and he would argue "long and ably" for any ideas that might promise a brighter future for this sport. "A grand champion, he was perhaps never so happy as when, chewing an unlit cigar, he participated in a game of pitch with a band of cronies in a room full of 'kibitzers' and amidst a running repartee between players and self-styled expert onlookers." Schulte was forced to retire in 1938 because of poor health but had the satisfaction of seeing one of his top track performers, Edwin Weir, succeed him. Weir was also an All-American football tackle at Nebraska. Pa kept his contacts with the university athletic program, gave timely advice when sought, and attended as many athletic events as his state of health permitted. The beloved coach passed away, October 18, 1944, but his spirit seems to hover over the Cornhusker field still.

The high esteem held for Nebraska's Grand Old Man was shown at the Big Seven Conference Track Meet in 1949. At that time the new field house was dedicated to his memory as the "Henry F. Schulte Field House." He was referred to as "a man whose greatness is legend; whose name and fame has never passed but has become an institution . . . whose name will be an inspiration in the days ahead." Many letters were received from Pa Schulte's pupils for a *Book of Memories* to be presented to Mrs. Schulte. These came from "small town businessmen and United States senators, doctors and coaches, successful and not too successful men in all walks of life." These letters came "not from the pen but from the heart, the hearts of the men who knew Henry Frank Schulte." Paul Zimmerman, sports editor of the *Los Angeles Times* and a former Nebraska trackman, wrote in part: "By his words, his smile, his deeds, he taught the thousands of us how to fairly play the game."

KARL STEFAN

My Congressman

MARCH 1, 1884 · OCTOBER 2, 1951

BOHEMIANS HAVE PLAYED an important role in the development of Nebraska. Settlements were made in many parts of the state by these talented and freedom loving people who left their native land to escape the oppression of the Hapsburgs. Czech names appear in every occupational and professional field in ever increasing numbers. Many of them hold responsible positions in public life on the local, state and national levels. None has been held in as high esteem in Nebraska as Karl Stefan who was elected nine consecutive times to serve the Third Nebraska District in Congress.

Edith Nourse Rogers, a congressional colleague, remarked: "It would be wonderful if every school in the country would have the history of Karl Stefan's life. What a fine thing, an inspiration, it would be for children to read; how good it would be for newcomers to this country." The story of "We Who Made Nebraska" would be incomplete, indeed, without the part played by this friend of mankind. Majority Leader McCormack of Massachusetts, his political foe, said: "Karl Stefan was loved by everyone who knew him—he had a calm and restrained mind." The *Norfolk* (Nebraska) *Daily News* editorialized:

"All who knew Karl Stefan instinctively felt that he was a personal friend. His public life had been built upon his rare ability to make friends. To his constituents Karl was not a 'Nebraska congressman,' or even 'our congressman.' He was to each individual 'my congressman.' This friendliness was not shown to his close acquaintances only. And it was not posed. . . . It was as natural to Karl as eating and breathing."

And Karl was not just a friendly person. He was a helpful one who used every device available, the press, radio, telephone, telegraph, public speaking apparatus, messenger service, and correspondence to serve his constituents. Had he lived longer there is no question but that he would have utilized television to good advantage. Once in the House Chamber he secretly "planted" microphones to prove their worth. The experiment proved quite a shock to some of his colleagues when their private conversations came booming over the loud speaker. The low-voiced members approved but the "loud-mouths" objected since these gadgets took away their advantage. Karl was a conscientious congressman and often became disgusted with the turn of events. "Not only did he work day and night to do what he felt should be done, like many other men in public life he had a feeling of frustration because he saw clearly what ought to be done, yet was unable to do it." Most of the time he spent in Washington the Republican party, to which he belonged, was on the defensive.

Karl, son of Karl and Marie Stefan, was born on a farm near the town of Zebrakov, Bohemia, March 1, 1884, just 17 years to the day after Nebraska became a state. Perhaps it was fate that the family, one year later, migrated to the United States and settled in Omaha. Here young Karl attended the public schools as well as the German and Bohemian parochial ones. Adept in learning foreign tongues he is said to have mastered thirteen during his lifetime. This proficiency stood him in well both in private and public life and put to shame some of his so-called educated colleagues who had difficulty in speaking one. Hard times forced Karl to quit school at the age of 13 when in the seventh grade but this merely spurred him on to educate himself in any way possible. He worked at various jobs: packing house, publicity department of the Trans-Mississippi Exposition scheduled for 1898, and as a messenger boy for Western Union. This latter job apparently gave him the incentive to learn telegraphy. He took night classes at the Y. M. C. A. and also lessons by correspondence and became one of the youngest and fastest telegraphers in the business.

With this trade he was now ready to satisfy an urge—to see his adopted country, and before his tour was ended he had worked as a travel-telegrapher in practically every state in the Union. Following this jaunt, while still in his teens, he sailed for the Far East to take a "look" at the Philippine Insurrection. He became a telegrapher for the Philippine Constabulary. For this and later services to the Filipinos he received many awards. He also did newspaper work for the *Manila Times,* his first venture in this field. Because of his linguistic ability he acted as an interpreter for world tourist parties. Returning to the United States he worked awhile on Omaha newspapers and on January 30, 1907, was married to Ida Rosenbaum. They moved to Seattle shortly where he worked as a telegrapher but apparently tired of the Northwest and returned to Nebraska, settling in Norfolk in 1909.

Norfolk was the ideal spot for Stefan. Here and throughout northeast Nebraska were people who responded to his friendliness. His ability to speak and visit with them in Bohemian, German or Scandinavian opened up channels denied most people. When Karl made a speech it was more in the nature of a visit than a platform talk. It was a personal thing and one who listened, whether in a hall or over the radio, had the feeling that he was speaking directly to him. Stefan's first job in Norfolk was that of telegrapher for the *Daily News* but later served, in addition, as city editor and chief news gatherer for the same paper. He resigned in 1924 when he bought a cigar store on Norfolk Avenue. There were lots of cigar stores but none like Karl's. It became a gathering place for the exchange of ideas. Telegraphic news, hot off the wires, appeared in his window where shoppers would stop to keep posted. He continued ownership of his store until shortly before his death, but it will probably always carry his name since it developed into a local institution.

Stefan had always been keenly interested in the development of new and faster means of communication. He was not only a telegrapher himself but taught the Morse and Continental codes to others. Wireless always intrigued him and when radio became an accepted fact he helped pioneer it into Norfolk. He assisted in setting up WJAG, the *Norfolk Daily News* station, in 1922 and until elected to Congress in 1934 was its chief announcer and newscaster. During these years he put Norfolk on the map but most of all he "sold" himself to the people, old and young, of northeast Nebraska. He originated many innovations, one of the most popular being the mythical radio family which he gathered around the imaginative table each noon. The old cowbell welcomed new babies; the daily hospital report would be made for the benefit of relatives and friends at home; "shut-in" funds were requested for purchasing radios for those bedfast; and information was given letting the folks at home know that "we got here all right."

He had a tremendous following in the early Twenties during world series games. A play-by-play account was taken from the wires and broadcast over WJAG. Another popular activity was the "Voice of the Street" program. He seemed to have something for everyone and his menu was especially pleasing to farm audiences. He also taught telegraphy by radio and awarded certificates to those who finished the course. After he went to Congress Karl made transcriptions of the "goings-on" in Washington which were then played over the Norfolk station. A regular report was likewise published in all the newspapers of the district. Few congressmen "nursed" their constituencies as did Karl Stefan. He was a regular "visitor" at local gatherings, such as county fairs, town festivals, "free days," and dedications.

The voters of northeast Nebraska paid little heed to party lines when Karl ran for Congress. In this respect he was like Senator Norris, but in Stefan's case it was more of a personal matter. In his first race he defeated the veteran Democrat Edgar Howard in a Democratic year, 1934, by a plurality of nearly 20,000 and polled more than 72,000 votes. In Congress he battled for the farmer and the small business man at every turn. But, because of his wide interests and his understanding of world affairs he became a sort of "trouble shooter" and international "ambassador of goodwill" during his long service. His most important assignment in the House was on the Appropriations Committee and he was ranking minority member at the time of his death. Had he lived a little longer he would have become the ranking majority member. He was especially concerned with the subcommittee handling of State and Justice Department spending. Though economy-minded, Stefan gave his fullest support to war appropriations but kept an eagle eye out to prevent waste and graft. A keen enthusiast over aviation Karl led the fight for the civilian pilot program. The field in Norfolk is named in his honor.

Just before World War II broke out Stefan was sent as an American delegate to the Inter-parliamentary Union at Oslo. While in Europe he inspected most of the United States service offices getting out just before the outbreak of war. In 1948, at the request of the House Committee on Appropriations, the Secretary of State and the Secretary of the Army, he made another survey of U. S. Foreign Service and Marshall Plan operations in Europe. His fluency in languages made Stefan a valuable man for many and varied missions throughout the world. He was an official adviser to the United Nations Conference in San Francisco in 1945 which adopted the United Nations charter, and his last official assignment was that of congressional observer at the signing of the Japanese peace treaty in San Francisco in September 1951. His report was made into a transcription for WJAG and was broadcast over that station after his death. In it he said:

"Congress AND the whole people should know the WHOLE truth about the Japanese peace treaty; not the partial truth. The treaty should not be approved hastily. Every paragraph, every sentence, every WORD must be carefully scrutinized to prevent the lot of the American people from becoming increasingly difficult to endure."

Karl believed that all international commitments should be brought out in the open. And he said that "the tragedy of San Francisco was and is that Gen. Douglas MacArthur—the prime factor in current good relations between Japan and the United States—was absent." He was bitter about the United States carrying 90 per cent of the load in Korea and feared we might find ourselves committed to repeat the cost in future Pacific wars.

Another note should be added on the use of Karl's abilities. During World War II he broadcast encouragement to the Filipinos and to his native Czechs in their own languages.

The high regard held for Karl Stefan is shown by the many honors and medals awarded him. Four Indian tribes, Omaha, Winnebago, Ponca and Santee Sioux adopted him as "Pah-Hug-Mon-Thee," meaning "Leader Man." He was presented the Cross of Eloy Alfaro for furthering inter-American relations. National University of Washington, D. C., granted him an honorary doctor of laws degree. The Philippine Commonwealth Government made him an honorary brigadier general and presented him with various medals. He was given honorary membership by the Spanish War Veterans and the Veterans of Foreign Wars.

That he led a busy life is demonstrated by his membership in many lodges and clubs such as Masons, Odd Fellows, Rotary, Lions, Elks, U.C.T., T.P.A., National Press Club, and the Army and Navy Club. An Episcopalian, he served the church as a vestryman for many years. Representative Taber of New York said: "I think Karl Stefan had a range of abilities as wide as any man I have known in this house." He was, as the *World-Herald* points out, "considerably more than a congressman who served his constituents well. He was a good American and a living success story, an immigrant from Bohemia who hustled and educated himself and made a success of several careers." And, to again quote the *Norfolk Daily News:* He stands "as an example of the fact that this country offers unlimited opportunties to those who are willing to work hard enough to deserve them."

ROBERT TAYLOR

(Spangler Arlington Brugh)

Versatile Actor

AUGUST 5, 1911

———◁◦▷———

A FILM STAR has certain obligations, according to Spangler
Arlington Brugh, better known as Robert Taylor. "There is a
certain duty to conduct yourself like a gentleman, to look well,
behave well and treat the public well." And, he adds: "I feel,
for instance, that I should have shaved today." He admits that
the attention showered on a movie celebrity sometimes becomes
irksome, "but thank God for my public—that's movie business."
Since 1934, the year he received his diploma from Pomona
College in Claremont, California, Robert has been in the movie
business. When "Magnificent Obsession" was released on New
Year's Eve, 1935, he suddenly became a star, the idol of the fans,
especially the fair sex. Under contract with MGM, Taylor was
loaned to Universal for the picture, playing opposite Irene

Dunne. Shortly after the premiere he attended President Roosevelt's birthday ball in Washington and in Baltimore was "mobbed by the fans," reminiscent of the days of Rudolph Valentino.

The next few years were to witness a repetition of this experience. He was the lover of the screen and played opposite many lovelies of the period. Exhibitors gave him fourth place as a box-office star in 1936 and one nation-wide poll placed him ahead of Clark Gable as the favorite male movie actor. His salary went up to $3,500 per week and his popularity brought him an avalanche of mail. Autographing pictures for his admirers took up his Sundays. Bob discovered that being an idol has its drawbacks but he did not flinch under the added burdens. The newspapers found much copy following his strenuous life, especially in his courtship of Barbara Stanwyck, whom he married in 1939. Hailed as a love-match that might last, it finally went the way of most Hollywood marriages, culminating in a friendly divorce in 1953. However, it lasted longer than that of most screen couples. Barbara is reported as still carrying a "torch" for Bob.

Robert Taylor, says Hedda Hopper, "is a Hollywood phenomenon. He's extremely modest, and after 18 years in pictures he seems embarrassed being called a star." Nebraskans like this quality in him and they, also, are pleased that he has not gone "highbrow." He visits his old haunts in the state frequently and calls on old friends who helped him on his way and who have applauded his successes. Recently in Omaha he was praised by the Strategic Air Command and given a citation for "emphasizing to the American public . . . the importance of strategic air power in the maintenance of world peace." This was in recognition for his excellent portrayal of Colonel Paul Tibbets, pilot of the first atom bomber, in a recent picture, "Above and Beyond."

But Robert Taylor is not just a synthetic service man. Early in 1943 he was sworn in as a lieutenant in the Navy's aviation transport division as S. A. Brugh. Thirty-two years of age, he was too old for combat flying so was made a flight instructor. In his training class he placed in the top fifth of the group. He must have been a fine instructor for he says none of his cadets "washed out." Before his discharge, late in 1945, Taylor directed seventeen training films and did the narration for the battle picture, "The Fighting Lady." In spite of being well known on the screen Bob says that he was seldom recognized while in the Navy. Certainly he sought no special favors and received none. Like Clark Gable and others he did his assignments and took his chances like anyone else.

Robert Taylor was born in Filley, Nebraska, August 5, 1911, and was christened Spangler Arlington by his parents, Spangler Andrew and Ruth Adelia Stanhope Brugh. Bob says his mother picked the "Arlington" from a lively novel she was reading. His father was a grain dealer but at the age of 30 took up the study of medicine. Mrs. Brugh was not well and he hoped he might help her regain her health. Apparently he succeeded for she is still living and resides in Hollywood in a home Bob bought for her some 15 years ago. It also has been her son's home much of the time since his divorce, a place where he can escape the movie crowd.

The Brugh family moved to Beatrice, Nebraska, not long after Arlington was born as it afforded better opportunities for practicing medicine and the boy's education. Dr. Brugh hoped his son would some day take over his practice but young "Doc" cared little for science and the smells of the laboratory. But, he did take to music, speech, and dramatics. He had a few lessons on the piano and tried the banjo and saxophone, but on the advice of his grade school orchestra teacher gave up these for the cello. In speech he excelled, winning the state championship and a ten-day trip to Detroit. But he was no "sissy" for he made the track team and his classmates elected him class president. He worked at part-time jobs while in school and during vacations shocked grain, clerked in a bank and did a variety of other things to earn his spending money.

Doane College in Crete, Nebraska, was his first college stop. He discovered once and for all, in his freshman year, that medicine was not for him. He tried economics but that, too, had no appeal. But music, oratory and dramatics were something else. He played the cello in a trio over a local radio station earning something toward his college expenses. Young Brugh took the lead in a play and, for a coonskin coat bribe by his mother, entered the oratorical contest. He won over three ministerial students and got the coat. While at Doane he sported a car, courtesy of Dad, on the promise of keeping his speed to 35 miles per hour. He was allowed 40 when he drove it to California on the heels of his music teacher, Herbert E. Gray, who had taken a position at Pomona College in Claremont. It proved to be a wise move for the handsome young collegian. He fell right into his niche at Pomona, taking the leads in several plays, studying oratory, and playing in the college orchestra. Talent scouts from Hollywood were on the prowl and the "Sheik" caught their eye when he played the part of Captain Stanhope in "Journey's End" early in 1934. Within two days his name was on a contract with MGM carrying a starting salary of thirty-five dollars a week. However, he stayed on at Pomona until graduation but, three times a week, he drove to Culver City to study under Oliver Hinsdell, MGM's dramatic coach. Later in the year his father died in Nebraska and after the funeral he brought his mother and grandmother to Hollywood to live.

Louis B. Mayer encouraged the young actor and also fixed him up with a new wardrobe—and a new name, Robert Taylor, which he legalized in 1942. His first effort was a small role in Will Rogers' "Handy Andy" on loan to Fox, but the days immediately ahead were to be busy ones. He played the lead in "Buried Loot" and a supporting part in "There's Always Tomorrow," and "A Wicked Woman." Fan mail began to roll in after "Society Doctor" in which he had the second lead. The year 1935 was a bright one for Bob. Supporting roles in "West Point of the Air" and "Times Square Lady" were followed by "Murder in the Fleet" in which he played opposite Jean Parker. Few movie actors have been seen on the screen with more feminine stars than Taylor. There was Irene Dunne in "Magnificent Obsession," Eleanor Powell in "Broadway Melody of 1936," Janet Gaynor in "Small Town Girl," Joan Crawford in "The Gorgeous Hussy," Loretta Young in "Private Number," Barbara Stanwyck in "His Brother's Wife," Greta Garbo in "Camille," and Jean Harlow in "Personal Property." He played opposite Hedy Lamarr in "Lady of the Tropics," Greer Garson in "Remember?," Myrna Loy in "Lucky Night," Norma Shearer in "Her Cardboard Lover," Vivien Leigh in "Waterloo Bridge," Ava Gardner in "The Bribe," Elizabeth Taylor in "Conspirator," Katharine Hepburn in "Under Current," and Deborah Kerr in "Quo Vadis." What movie star could ask for more? And, the list is incomplete.

Bob has taken many roles besides that of the ordinary screen lover. He has been a fighter, an aviator, mule driver, killer, naval and army officer, an industrialist, mental patient, secret service man, frontiersman, Indian, Roman centurion, trail boss and medieval knight. In "Bataan" he was a "hard-bitten" ser-

[180]

geant. "Quo Vadis," in which Taylor portrays the part of Marcus Vinicius the Roman centurion, was made in Italy and required his presence there most of 1950. Though not too well received by the critics it was a "supercolossal" spectacle. In addition to the leading actors and actresses there were in the cast: "30,000 Italian extras, 63 lions . . . seven bulls, 450 horses, two cheetahs, 85 white doves, 10 hogs (for the sacrificial altar) and five teams of oxen. There were 115 scenes, including reproduction of three blocks of the ancient city of Rome and a replica of the huge Circus of Nero, and 150,000 props, and 32 thousand costumes. Yup, Bob Taylor drives a chariot." Recent pictures starring the busy actor include: "Westward the Women," "Ivanhoe," and "Above and Beyond."

Spangler Arlington Brugh has packed a lot of exciting experiences into his life since he left the little Nebraska village of Filley. He may not stir feminine hearts as he once did but he is still not out of the running. Almost every day brings fresh rumors of a new romance. But, Bob seems to like the bachelor life he leads at present. Fishing, hunting, skeet shooting, collecting model racing cars, breeding field dogs and horses, and flying his own six-passenger plane take up some of his "spare" time. This six-footer, weighing 175 pounds and conservatively dressed, makes a handsome appearance with his dark hair slightly sprinkled with gray and set off with a sporty moustache. He says he enjoys doing "Westerns" best and that Billy the Kid is a favorite role. Like many movie actors, Taylor thinks he "stinks" in most of his pictures. Judging by the box-office his public does not agree. No wonder he says: "Thank God for my public."

GEORGE FRANCIS TRAIN

Promoter

MARCH 24, 1829 · JANUARY 18, 1904

GEORGE FRANCIS TRAIN was one of the most intriguing characters to set foot on Nebraska soil. In many respects he was a remarkable figure. He is remembered best as a dispenser of ballyhoo. Train has been described as a genius, brilliant organizer, champion of causes, advertiser deluxe, prophet, charming speaker, entertaining writer and successful merchant. He has, likewise, been labeled by the iconoclasts as a "wind-bag," "hot-air artist," "liar," and a notorious swindler of the first order. The truth probably lies somewhere between these points of view. At any rate he stirred up considerable dust in territorial Nebraska and enlivened many a gathering with his glib tongue and Irish humor.

Train had just returned from Europe when the stage was being set for building the Union Pacific railroad. Already he had established a reputation as a brilliant stump speaker. Though

[182]

only 33 when he first visited Omaha he had seen much of the world. Possessing a prodigious memory he was said to be "an encyclopedia of all knowledge, a walking library" and as probably having a "larger fund of knowledge than any man in America." An added comment, however, stated that the "Train of ideas sometimes lack the coupling chains." In London he had tried to promote the introduction of street cars. He had, also, interested English capital in the construction of the Atlantic and Western Railway. His mercantile interests reached into all parts of the world and the title of "globe trotter" had been conferred upon him.

While in Europe Train spoke out boldly in support of the North in the War of the Rebellion. He delivered over 100 speeches on this theme in Great Britain and Ireland. Upon returning to the United States in 1862 he went on a lecture tour which almost ended disastrously for him. He was shot at in Dayton, Ohio, arrested and ordered out of Missouri, barely escaped assassination in Alton, Illinois, and was bayoneted at Davenport, Iowa. But his Irish luck stayed with him. Late that year he began the organization of the Kansas Pacific railroad. Promoting was his dominant interest. About this time Thomas C. Durant was developing plans for building a transcontinental railroad. He needed a man like Train in his schemes and induced the young optimist to join him in promoting the financing of the Union Pacific, of which he was vice president. It was a clever move, for this versatile man of the world knew his way around. He took the lead in securing a charter for the Credit Mobilier, an inside corporation that did the actual construction. Train knew the "right" people and the stock was distributed where it would have the most telling effects politically.

Immediately following Lincoln's proclamation locating the starting point of the road Train, at Durant's suggestion, hastened to Omaha and took a leading part in the ground-breaking ceremony. Here on December 2, 1863, he closed the exercises with a rousing speech, sparkling with wit, in which he made extravagant predictions regarding the future of the Union Pacific. One newspaper described it as the "raciest, liveliest, best natured, and most tip-top speech ever delivered west of the Missouri." The people who heard him thought his prophecies overdrawn but in less than six years his forecasts had come true.

George Francis Train was born in Boston, Massachusetts, March 24, 1829. At the age of 4 he went with his parents to New

Orleans. Almost immediately his father, mother and three sisters died of yellow fever. George Francis was then sent back to New England where he lived with a grandmother until he was 12. His formal education consisted of only three months' attendance but he was adept at schooling himself. From the age of 12 his career runs a story book pattern. At that time he took a job in a grocery store. At 15 he became chief clerk for a shipping concern and at 19 established the house of Train and Company in Liverpool. Here he organized a "prepaid passenger business throughout Europe and America." But Train believed in expanding. The same year, 1849, he tied in as one of the proprietors of the Diamond Line of Liverpool and New York that sailed packets to many world ports. In 1850 he became a partner in the Enoch Train and Company in Boston with full management of the business. He was married the following year to the beautiful Willie Davis, daughter of Colonel George T. Davis of Louisville, Kentucky.

Train was not content to stay cooped up in an office. His next venture was in Australia where he founded a large store and warehouse in Melbourne, organized a chamber of commerce and board of trade, and stimulated interest in a railroad to extend from Melbourne to Sandridge. He was even offered the presidency, in 1853, of a proposed Australian republic which some revolutionaries hoped to establish, but declined. Returning to England in 1858 he proceeded to champion a street railway system there. Failing to get support from Parliament he did, by consent of the road authorities, lay tramways in Birkenhead and London.

It is said that Train made five trips around the world during his lifetime, doing one in 80 days. His "round-the-world speeches" were corkers. He summarized his last trip in this fashion: "I bulldozed the Mikado in Japan, frightened out of their wits the Chinese at Hong Kong, bewildered the Malays at Singapore, ran over the Singalese in Ceylon, drove the Arabs crazy at Aden, astonished the Italians, French, English, and Irish in turn, in a rapid rush through Europe, and returned to the United States." He might just as well have added that he gave the Americans the "bums' rush."

Omaha appealed to Train as a good spot to try out his promoting talents. Sometimes he did things to satisfy a desire for revenge. Such a move was the building of the Cozzens House, a hotel which he had constructed in two months to spite the manager of the Herndon House. The story goes that Train was eating dinner at this hotel and was paying a Negro waiter ten cents a minute to block the draft from a broken window. The manager ordered the waiter away and this angered Train who forthwith bought a lot across the street and proceeded, post haste, to put up a rival hotel. The money for this $40,000 structure is said to have been furnished by a wealthy New Haven jeweler and was rented to the Cozzens Company of New York. It became one of the best known hotels in the west.

Train was also involved in some real estate deals in Omaha. In 1865 he purchased 500 acres of land in the southeast part of the city. He took 80 acres of this and plotted it into lots naming the area Credit Foncier Addition. This was paid for but the remainder was lost through foreclosure. He always boasted that he owned city lots in Omaha worth $30,000,000. Train was always on the move but "popped up" in Omaha often enough to create some excitement there. Usually a cordial reception was extended him. One writer comments: "He was graceful as a dancing master, was a dandy in his dress, invariably wore a flower in his lapel, and always presented a neat and handsome appearance. He was a man of ready wit, cutting sarcasm, and quick repartee." Once when Train was in Omaha to deliver a lecture the local distiller, Peter Iler, charged him with being an anarchist. In his lecture the speaker said: "My fellow citizens, I have been informed that Peter Iler has referred to me as an anarchist, and in reply allow me to say that there is more anarchy in one barrel of Peter Iler's whisky than there is in 10,000 George Francis Trains."

Time and time again his enemies tried to "get something on him" and it is said he was jailed seventeen times. But, he was never convicted of any crimes so spent very little time in jail. His writings, started in 1857, were mostly on the entertaining level and the titles give some insight to his interests and experiences. Some of these are: *An American Merchant in Europe, Asia and Australia; Young America Abroad; Young America in Wall Street; Spread-Eagleism; Young America on Slavery; Irish Independency; Championship of Women; Observations on Street Railways;* and *My Life in Many States and Foreign Lands.*

One of the most thrilling episodes in the life of George Francis Train was the premiere of the opening of the Union Pacific Railroad to the region of North Platte, Nebraska. A party of notables, including several congressmen and railroad officials, left New York, October 23, 1866, and arrived in Omaha less than a week later. Since there was no railroad within 56 miles to the east of Omaha the last leg of the journey was by boat. Omaha, the territorial capital, was twelve years old and had a population of 10,000. It was now boasting of being the Gateway to the West and went all out to welcome the visitors. They were royally entertained at a reception and ball at the Herndon House. Governor Alvin Saunders, Mayor Lorin Miller and all the top territorial officials were on hand. "The guests danced, promenaded and partook of excellent and substantial refreshments till 2 o'clock in the morning." Before leaving on their excursion the party visited the addition plotted by the Credit Foncier, "that remarkable land company headed by Mr. Train and designed to promote towns along the great national highway."

There were six coaches on the trip west. The Trains rode in Durant's private car along with the Dodges and other dignitaries. This was the "famous Lincoln funeral train car" but a much different atmosphere prevailed on this occasion. Mrs. Train was singled out by an editor as a "beautiful woman and one of the belles of the excursion party" and "one of the most perfect ladies we have had the honor to meet." The party reached Columbus at 7 P.M. the first day and spent the night there in "a city of tents." Pawnee Indians entertained them with songs and dances for two hours. The visitors walked about the town (population about 200) which Mr. Train predicted would become the capital of the nation. They, also, witnessed a sham battle at the Indian encampment led by one of the famous North brothers.

The next evening encampment was made at Brady's Island, 275 miles from Omaha. They dubbed the camp Platte City, alias Durant. After dinner that night there were songs and speeches with Mr. Train presiding. From this point some of the party made huntng trips guarded by soldiers from Fort McPherson. The end of the line was reached the next day and the visitors were amazed at the system of laying track at the rate of one and a half miles a day. Someone suggested a celebration. The excursionists, in a gay mood, responded lustily with dances, speeches and songs.

"We're bound to ride all night,
We're bound to ride all day.
We've bet our cash on the U. P. R.
Somebody bet where he may."

This and many other songs rang across the prairie. "As subjects were suggested to him George Francis Train improvised the verses, and he and Mrs. Train sang them. A reporter who sent his dispatch from this point said that Train had made 2,575 verses and was still going strong." A fireworks display and band concert followed the sumptuous dinner (42 items on the menu). Many pictures were taken. On the return trip the group saw a prairie fire 15 miles long—arranged by Durant.

George Francis Train did a great deal of "politicking" but was never considered seriously for office. He did not stay "put" long enough. In 1866 he entered the race for delegate to Congress as an Independent after the Democrats failed to nominate him. A list of 31 Irishmen was published urging him to remain in the contest. They said they favored him because he had "advocated so long the cause of Irish nationality" and "has already done and is now doing more for the future advancement of Nebraska than any other man, or set of men has done for it since it was organized as a territory." This picturesque figure made several campaign speeches which were described as lacking coherency but "wonderfully bright, drool, witty, sarcastic, and humorous" as contrasted with his opponents. Train, however, withdrew from the race and in a characteristic letter said: "When men emancipate themselves from party, when voters regain their independence, when the people of Nebraska are more anxious to have me for their representative than I am to represent them, when an election can be carried without purchase, perhaps I may enter the field again."

Train has been called an "eccentric genius," a kind-hearted person who throughout a long and eventful career never harmed a soul. As a lover of children and birds he had few equals spending "hours with them in the parks of New York City, when, for weeks at a time, he would not converse with grown people." George D. Prentice, writing in the *Louisville Courier Journal*, gives a not-so-complimentary but highly descriptive appraisal of Train:

"A locomotive that has run off the track, turned upside down, with its cow-catcher buried in a stump, and the wheels making a thousand revolutions a minute—a kite in the air, which has lost its tail—a human novel without a hero—a man who climbs a tree for a bird's nest out on a limb, and in order to get it saws off the limb between himself and the tree—a ship without a rudder—a clock without hands—a sermon that is all text—a pantomime of words—an arrow shot into the air—the apotheosis of talk—the incarnation of gab—handsome, vivacious, versatile, muscular—as neat as a cat— clean to the marrow—a judge of the effect of clothes—frugal in food and regular only in habits—a noonday mystery—a solved conun- drum—a practical joke in earnest—a cipher hunting a figure to pass for something—with the brains of twenty men in his head all pull- ing different ways—not bad as to heart, but a man who has shaken hands with reverence."

Mr. Train summarized his life career in his own inimitable way as follows:

"Born at No. 21 High Street, Boston, 1829; residence Continen- tal hotel, at present; generally in some jail; color, octoroon; sex, male; height, five feet eleven inches. My father was born in Boston, my mother at Waltham, Mass. My room, bed, desk in our home- stead, two hundred years old, are still shown to visitors. Married in 1851. My wife is dead. My education was had in three months at a winter school. I am strictly temperate; I never tasted liquor. I have three grown-up children."

Charles A. Dana once said of him, "He is living 200 years ahead of his time; yet until he is dead the fact will never be known."

George Francis Train may not have been an admirable char- acter. He had many faults and some of his "deals" bordered on the shady side. But, he was in tune with the times. Many public officials of his day were involved in graft and it is too much to expect one as ingenious as he to pass up an opportunity for easy money. But in spite of personal greed, or because of it, he alerted people to the possibilities of the West and stimulated a spirit of optimism in them. He made the future look bright to the citi- zens of the young commonwealth of Nebraska.

DARRYL ZANUCK

Movie Tycoon

SEPTEMBER 5, 1902

———◆———

NEBRASKA HAS CONTRIBUTED many stars to the movie industry but the man who has helped make them shine is a bundle of energy called Darryl Zanuck. An 18-hour day worker, he is aptly described as a human dynamo. His terrific zeal and careful planning have given us an almost endless run of great pictures. His imagination knows no boundaries. A visit to his offices is almost awe-inspiring with the array of medals, trophies and awards, including Oscars that adorn the place. His display goes beyond the movie scene for Zanuck is a big game hunter of some consequence. He loves the strenuous life, both on and off the movie lot. One of his colleagues, William Wellman, recalls a trip with him to British Columbia: "It snowed. We had to break trail for the horses. We were snowbound for three days. Zanuck chased a grizzly for 30 hours, came back with a sprained ankle. We lost

[189]

the horse carrying our medicine. I got blood poisoning. It was the ruggedest trip you've ever seen. But Zanuck loved it."

Cornhuskers will boast that only a state with variable weather patterns like Nebraska could produce a character with such tough fibre as this energetic fireball of Hollywood. Born in Wahoo, Nebraska, September 5, 1902, of Swiss and English parentage he hardly waited to grow up before starting his restless career. His father operated a grain elevator and the local hotel. Young Zanuck had an opportunity to meet people and pick up ideas. While Darryl was still a youngster the family moved to Glendale, California, but the lad had some history to make before he settled in that land of promise. At the age of 15, when most boys were starting to high school, he talked (or lied) his way into the Nebraska National Guard. He spent two years in service, on the Mexican border and in France, thus becoming a veteran at the age of 17.

School was too confining for his restless spirit. His formal education ended with the 8th grade. He was determined to be an author and set to work, writing furiously, but met with poor success selling his product. He moved to California in 1922 where he shuttled about trying his hand at several jobs including a stint in a shipyard and several selling efforts. Unperturbed by setbacks young Zanuck, cocky as a rooster, went all-out to conquer Hollywood. He made a pest of himself at the Athletic Club in Los Angeles where the bigwigs hung out. He got a few "breaks" and was successful in disposing of his stories until the studios toughened up on free-lancers without literary reputations. He had to "do" a book or else. His production, *Habit,* was actually a compilation of three of his rejected scenarios put in narrative form and embellished with a chapter ballyhooing a certain hair tonic, the manufacturer of which paid for the printing. He used it, also, to impress the lovely Virginia Fox with whom he had fallen in love. His ardent wooing paid off for she became Mrs. Zanuck in 1924 and has since been a balance wheel in his life.

These were the silent screen days but talkies were on the horizon. He became associated with Warners in 1924 and helped pull them out of the red with his clever stories centered around the famous dog star, Rin-Tin-Tin, resulting in a run of popular box office attractions. Zanuck really let himself go in devising unusual things for the dog to do. He became general production manager in 1929, jumping his salary from $125 to

$5000 a week, and was gaining a reputation as "somebody" in Hollywood. He blossomed out with a bright green Rolls Royce and "green" soon became a sort of trademark with him which to this day is his favorite color. He went in for polo in a big way and became the owner of a string of ponies. He said he needed the exercise. 1933 brought the New Deal in Washington and it brought a new deal for Zanuck. After a tiff with Harry Warner he quit that studio and hied himself to Joseph M. Schenck of United Artists for advice on his next move. The two worked out a deal resulting in the formation of Twentieth Century. Short on assets but long in optimism, Schenck, Zanuck, and a screen writer, Nunally Johnson, worked with a vengeance. Within 18 months, 18 pictures were made and by 1935 the upstart company looked like a major concern. George Arliss had been about their only initial star.

The Fox Film Corporation was a well-padded company financially but needed someone to build a fire under it to bring its earnings up to par. Zanuck was such a man. In August, 1935, a merger was effected by the two studios creating Twentieth Century-Fox. With ample revenue and stars such as Shirley Temple and Will Rogers, the Dynamo, now ensconced as vice president in charge of production, went into action and the earnings of the new company soared. The next six years brought Zanuck into his own. A rapid succession of pictures "designed to enlighten as well as entertain" rolled from the studios of Twentieth Century-Fox.

With the coming of World War II Zanuck became more and more involved in the international scene. He supervised the production of training films for our defense forces. Made a lieutenant colonel in the Signal Corps in 1941 and a colonel in 1942, he came into contact with world leaders through his job as co-ordinator of Allied photographic activities. Churchill, Eden, Clark, and Truman were only a few of these. A giant cigar smoker he still exchanges stogies with Churchill. He served in the North African theater of operations and was awarded the Legion of Merit for his war service. 1943 found him back on the studio lot, an "eager beaver" all set to put the cameras to work on new themes involving the spirit of the new age, even though some were of a controversial nature.

This pioneer, this blazer of trails, this man of imagination has no peers in Hollywood. Never reluctant to take chances he is usually a couple of jumps ahead of his competitors. Daring, defiant, dazzling, and domineering at times, Zanuck keeps his staff in a dither. With his underlings on the hop the pot boils. The wand waving wizard of the cinema has a full day, indeed. A chain smoker (he consumes 20 cigars a day), Zanuck crams phone calls, dictation, production schedules, conferences, reports, and a multitude of other business into a day that seldom ends for him until 2 to 4 A.M. He, grudgingly, finds time to eat but business may accompany the process. His wife and three children frequently dine with him at the studio around 8 P.M. Before this, however, he has had a rubdown and a nap in a soundproof room back of his office. He does, somehow, sandwich in time to relax at his luxurious beach house as well as entertain his friends. Long week-ends and annual six-weeks' trips abroad help him to keep up this frantic pace. But, much of his work goes with him and he keeps in close touch with Hollywood.

Television has presented a serious threat to his interests but Zanuck is not frightened by it. He doesn't scare easily. He believes that quality pictures will stand up against this interloper. Change is part of his life and he has met the challenge many times. He has the knack of making the most out of new innovations and turning seeming obstacles into opportunities.

Zanuck's outstanding productions make up an exceedingly long list. Among these are: "Little Caesar," "Public Enemy," "Five Star Final," "I Am a Fugitive from a Chain Gang," "The Jazz Singer," "House of Rothschild," "Les Miserables," "Cardinal Richelieu," and "Wilson." Others worthy of mention are: "How Green Was My Valley," "Forever Amber," "Grapes of Wrath," "Gentlemen's Agreement," "Snake Pit," "Pinky," "Razor's Edge," "Winged Victory," "This Above All," "The Purple Heart," and "Twelve O'Clock High." But the list could go on and on. And, the end is not in sight.

That Darryl Zanuck is a remarkable person no one can deny. The "wheels" in his head are perfectly synchronized and the timing is perfect. He never heard of the term inferiority complex. A more confident or optimistic character never lived. This medium sized man of 50 years (weight 142 pounds, height about 5 feet, 7 inches), is not only a glutton for work but with his unbounded energy has the "know-how" to get things done. His example is contagious. Undoubtedly, many producers envy his film productivity. In a recent interview with the initimable Hedda Hopper, Zanuck presented the following as part of his formula for making successful pictures: "A producer must guess right. There are certain known ingredients. First you must have a story that reaches you emotionally. A successful picture, big or small, has to make you do one of three things: Sit on the edge of your seat, laugh a lot, or reach for your handkerchief." Wahoo's gift to Hollywood has made us do all three.

BIBLIOGRAPHICAL NOTES

THE DATA used for writing these sketches has come from a variety of materials. Since these characterizations are not definitive in scope but rather in the nature of summarizations, there has been no planned effort to cite specific sources in the text. However, the writer wishes to express his appreciation to all who have made this information available, and to those who have lent encouragement to the project. The following represents, in part, the sources consulted:

1. NEWSPAPERS:

Clippings collected over a period of years have been of inestimable value. These have been taken from a number of dailies including the *Omaha World-Herald, Lincoln Star, Nebraska State Journal, Columbus Daily Telegram, Norfolk Daily News, Scottsbluff Daily Star-Herald, Denver Post* and the *New York Sunday Times.* Other papers such as the *Nebraska Farmer,* the *Commoner* and several weeklies have also been used. The verses in the Bryan story were taken from a poem, "The Burials of Bryan," by Dudley Reid and appeared in the *Osceola* (Iowa) *Tribune,* July 30, 1925. Special credit is due the *World-Herald,* a principal source. The editor of this newspaper, W. E. Christenson, has generously permitted liberal quotation from this publicaion. It would be impossible to single out each contributor as many articles have appeared without the authors' names. However, included in the list of writers are the following: Max Coffey, Ted Landale, Lawrence Youngman, Doris Minney, Don W. Sigler, Frederick Ware, Floyd Olds, Gregg McBride, Claire Conley, Robert Houston, Jay Monaghan, Ken Keller, Vernon Hoyt, Edward Morrow. Credit is also due James E. Lawrence, editor of the *Lincoln Star,* especially for an article on Roscoe Pound and to Zela H. Loomis, general manager of the *Columbus Telegram,* for detailed information on Edgar Howard. Editorials, giving appraisals of some of the people in this book, have been very helpful.

2. MAGAZINES:

Many periodicals, carrying biographical sketches or comments on Nebraskans included in this book, have been utilized. Some of these are: *Life, Time, Fortune, Newsweek, Current History, Reader's Digest, Coronet, Look, Saturday Review of Literature, Collier's, American Magazine, Good Housekeeping, Parents' Magazine, Pathfinder, Saturday Evening Post, Nation's Business, Nation, New Republic, U. S. News and World Report, Survey, Music America* and a number of historical journals such as *Nebraska History* and the *Mississippi Valley Historical Review.* The editors of *Life* have granted permission to quote from Robert Wallace's article, "Herbert Brownell, Eisenhower's Right Hand," December 22, 1952, copyright *Time* Inc. 1952, and from an article, "Herbert Brownell, Jr., The Cabinet: Eighth of a Series," April 6, 1953, copyright *Time* Inc. 1953. *Life* has also given permission to quote from Robert Coughlan's article, "Al Gruenther, The Thinking Machine Who Bosses NATO," June 1, 1953, copyright *Time* Inc. 1953. The editors of *Time* have allowed quotations from the story on Darryl Zanuck, "One Man Studio," June 12, 1950, copyright *Time* Inc. 1950, and from articles on Robert Taylor appearing in that magazine May 22, 1939, January 17, 1944, April 7, 1947, November 3, 1947, copyright *Time* Inc. 1939, 1944 and 1947 respectively. These courtesies on the part of the editors are deeply appreciated.

3. CORRESPONDENCE AND INTERVIEWS:

Letters from the following individuals have supplied much useful information: Chris Abbott, Hyannis; Guy Chamberlin, Lincoln; John R. Jirdon, Morrill; Mrs. H. F. Schulte, Minneapolis, Minnesota; B. B. Miltonberger, North Platte; Walt Dobbins, Lincoln; Floyd Olds, Omaha; Mrs. G. G. Eisenhart, McCook; E. F. Pettis, Omaha; Msgr. Nicholas H. Wegner, Boys Town; B. J. Scannell, Omaha; Zela H. Loomis, Columbus; Mr. and Mrs. Paul C. Gallagher, Omaha; W. G. Murphy, Omaha; Edgar Howard, Columbus; George "Potsy" Clark, Lincoln; Louise Pound, Lincoln; Karl Stefan, Norfolk; Sam McKelvie, Valentine; Charles Segar, New

York City. Several interviews have, likewise, added to the data. Special credit should go to Lillian Wadsworth of Tilden, Nebraska, who carried on some of the correspondence and to Ardith Boumann of Norfolk, for assembling considerable material on Nebraska women.

4. PAMPHLETS:

A varied collection of pamphlets, booklets, brochures, abstracts, bulletins, journals, reports, special programs and scrapbooks have furnished information, much of which is of a biographical nature. The librarians of the Nebraska State Historical Society, the Nebraska Library Commission and the Omaha Public Library have been very cooperative, as have the Wayne State Teachers College and Wayne City librarians. O. R. Bowen, Professor Emeritus of Wayne State Teachers College, has generously given the writer various materials dealing with Nebraska history and Nebraska personalities.

5. ENCYCLOPEDIAS, DICTIONARIES, YEARBOOKS, DIRECTORIES:

A number of these have been used in checking factual data, chronological sequence, etc. Among those used are the following: *Who's Who in America; Who's Who in the Midwest; Who's Who in American Education; Congressional Directory; Nebraska Blue Book; Who's Who in Nebraska; The American Scholar; American Men of Science; American Composers of Today; Twentieth Century Authors; Information Please Almanac; National Cyclopaedia of American Biography; Dictionary of American Biography; Current Biography.* Brief quotations have been taken from the last three works for which the writer wishes to extend due credit.

6. BOOKS:

There are numerous books that deal with various phases and periods of Nebraska history and the people who helped make that history. Many county histories are available, some of which are very useful. However, none of these will be listed here for lack of space. A few general works, autobiographies, and biographies follow:

Andreas, A. T., *History of the State of Nebraska,* Chicago, 1882.
Bennett, Mildred R., *The World of Willa Cather,* New York, 1951.
Bryan, William Jennings and Mary Baird, *The Memoirs of William Jennings Bryan,* Chicago, 1925.
Carmichael, John P. and Other Sports Writers, *My Greatest Day in Baseball,* New York, 1945.
Cody, William F., *Autobiography of Buffalo Bill,* New York, 1920.
Dick, Everett N., *The Sod House Frontier, 1854–1890,* New York, 1937.

BIBLIOGRAPHICAL NOTES

Department of Athletics, University of Nebraska, *Spotlighting the Husker Greats* (Booklet), Lincoln, 1951. Included is Walt Dobbins' "Spotlighting 50 Years of Husker Football."

Johnson, Harrison, *History of Nebraska,* Omaha, 1880.

Lowry, Edward G., *Washington Close-Ups,* New York, 1921.

Morton, J. Sterling and Watkins, Albert, *Illustrated History of Nebraska,* 3 vols., Lincoln, 1905–13.

Neuberger, Richard L. and Kahn, Stephen B., *Integrity; the Life of George W. Norris,* New York, 1937.

Norris, George W., *Fighting Liberal, Autobiography of George W. Norris,* New York, 1945.

Olson, James C., *J. Sterling Morton,* Lincoln, 1942.

Oursler, Fulton and Will, *Father Flanagan of Boys Town,* New York, 1949.

Owen, Steve, *My Kind of Football,* New York, 1952.

Palmer, Frederick, *John J. Pershing, General of the Armies,* Harrisburg, Pa., 1948.

Pershing, John Joseph, *My Experiences in the World War,* New York, 1931.

Riegel, Robert, *America Moves West,* New York, 1947.

Sawyer, Andrew J., *Lincoln, the Capital City and Lancaster County, Nebraska,* Chicago, 1916.

Sayre, Paul, *The Life of Roscoe Pound,* Iowa City, 1948.

Scherman, David E. and Redlick, Rosemarie, *Literary America,* New York, 1952.

Ware, Frederick and McBride, Gregg, *Fifty Years of Football, A Condensed History of the Game at the University of Nebraska* (Booklet), Omaha, 1940.